(as part of the package)

The Spirit Comes

(as part of the package)

Why being charismatic is not an option

John Leach

Marshall Pickering
An Imprint of HarperCollins*Publishers*

Zondervan
P.O. Box 749, Harrow HA1 1DP, UK
Grand Rapids, Michigan 49530, USA

First published in Great Britain and the USA in 2001 by
Zondervan

1 3 5 7 9 10 8 6 4 2

A catalogue record for this book is available
from the British Library.

ISBN 0 00 710362 X

Printed and bound in Great Britain by
Omnia Books Limited, Glasgow

Without the Holy Spirit:
    God is far away,
    Christ stays in the past,
    the Gospel is a dead letter,
    the church is simply an organisation,
    authority a matter of domination,
    mission a matter of propaganda,
    the liturgy no more than an evocation,
    Christian living a slave morality.

But in the Holy Spirit:
    The cosmos is resurrected
    and groans with the birth-pangs of the kingdom,
    the risen Christ is there,
    the Gospel is the power of life,
    the church shows forth the life of the Trinity,
    authority is a liberating service,
    mission is a Pentecost,
    the liturgy is both memorial and anticipation
    human action is deified.

(Attributed to
Metropolitan Ignatios
of Latakia, 1968)

Contents
. . . .

Why Should I Read This Book?

The Christian Church today is made up of many different bits. Denominations, such as Anglican, Baptist or Methodist; parties, such as Evangelicals or Liberals; churchmanships, like 'High Church' or 'Low Church': all these and many more engage in gentle and polite competition for our attention as we seek to live out our Christian discipleship within the Body of Christ. This book is not about any of these parties or groupings: it is about another one, known as the 'charismatic movement', or the 'renewal'. Most of us have encountered renewal somewhere or other, either personally or through the media, and we may even have 'signed up' personally and become 'members' of this movement. I'll be telling you my story in the next chapter: yours may be similar, and it may or may not have ended as happily as mine did.

Some recent history

When charismatic renewal hit the British church in the mid sixties, different people reacted to it in different ways. Some embraced it gladly and immediately as a promised new move of God. They found that it fulfilled scripture, and on a personal level it restored in them a sense of joy and refreshment in spiritual dryness. The culture around it, particularly that of its worship, was welcomed and valued, and many people testified to a new depth in their spirituality, a new power and authority in their ministry, a new love of prayer and the Bible, and the satisfying of a thirst for a deeper personal relationship with God. Others, like me, embraced it slowly, painfully and with great hesitation. It hurt, but we did get there in the end. But still others were nowhere near as convinced, and reacted with enduring hostility to all things charismatic, for a whole variety of reasons.

Opponents of renewal saw this new movement as theologically questionable, somewhere on a spectrum between misguided and downright heretical. They found its worship subjective and senti-mental, its claims of the miraculous as spurious and unproven, and its exhibitionism embarrassing. They set about collecting stories of Bad Experiences – not always a difficult task – Bad Experiences which were so significant that one felt they had to be spelled with a capital 'B' and 'E', stories of unbalanced people being sent danger-ously over the top, or of those devastated because promises of healing or other victories were not fulfilled. Some saw the expositors of renewal as playing fast and loose with scripture, using personal experience as a greater authority than the written Word of God. Earnest pastors preached to their congregations about the profound dangers of dabbling in such spirituality, as though it were on a par with the most rampant occultism. Some, indeed, felt that it was.

There were, of course, genuine Bad Experiences, in both direc-tions. Those who were young in the renewal movement often took on an arrogant or patronizing attitude towards those who had not had an experience of 'baptism in the Spirit', treating them as though they belonged to some kind of inferior class of Christians. Those who had a high degree of gifting from the Spirit but not enough maturity of character to handle it ministered to others in some very unhelpful ways, seeing demons everywhere and attempt-ing to drive out 'spirits of flu' or whatever, or making extravagant promises of healing which they could not in the end fulfil. Many, many people became frustrated with their churches, where their new-found experience of the Spirit was ignored or even preached directly against, and left to find more conducive fellowship. When individuals left churches it was damaging, but when a significant-sized group departed at one go churches were left devastated. And, of course, it was always charismatic renewal which was to blame, and never the closed or hostile attitude of the rest of the church towards charismatic renewal. 'This can't be the Spirit at work,' so the rhetoric went, 'since the Spirit is the Spirit of unity. He wouldn't do anything to divide a church!' In fact the phrase only occurs once in the Bible, in Romans 15:5, where the context and the lack of a capital 'S' for 'spirit' make it clear that this is not a reference to the Holy Spirit at all, but rather a prayer that unity might characterize the life of the church. However, it is always a mistake to expect critics to confuse their rhetoric with the facts! My understanding is that the Holy Spirit always divides: he divides those who are willing to follow Jesus from those who are not.

Those who did stay put in their churches were often accused, not without some justification, of being cliquey or élitist: their secret goings-on in home groups or charismatic prayer cells became the subject of intense speculation and gossip among those who would not in a million years think of going along themselves to find out what really happened.

A few years into renewal the House Churches began to spring to life around the country. Typically a small group of charismatics, frustrated by the cold reception they received at their mainstream churches, would begin to meet together instead in someone's front room, to enjoy the kind of worship, fellowship and ministry for which their new-found relationship with the Spirit made them crave, free from the constraints of liturgy, 'churchianity' or tradition. These groups grew, coalesced into different streams, and, having been born out of splits, began themselves to split and re-form with predictable regularity. 'Commitment' and 'doing one's duty' became things of the past, and consumerism ruled: God wants me to be where the blessings are. The rhetoric of the early pioneers of the House Church movement about God's judgement being meted out on the denominations hasn't come to pass yet, but people really believed it at the time, and the hostility of some charismatics towards the heritage of established denominational churches is as strong today, although they are often from within those denominations.

And of course, like any movement, the charismatic renewal had and still has its loony fringe. Those within the renewal no doubt regard some of those on the edge as a great embarrassment, and might want to dissociate themselves from their views, but those on the other side love them because they can write them off – and the whole movement along with them – as being one chorus short of a songbook. Political parties often attract such extremists around their margins: were you to ask any prime minister, I'm sure they would be able to name some whom they would not regard as truly reflecting party policy, while members of the opposition with a mind to could point at those same people in order to prove how evil and misguided the party in power is if it holds views like *that*!

Charismatic renewal has some strange views around its margins: a preoccupation with the demonic, or the health and wealth promises of the prosperity gospel, or an anti-intellectual naïvety, to name but three. Many use those fringes to allow them to write off the movement as a whole, even though mainstream renewal people would be just as unhappy with them and just as keen to dissociate themselves from them. We shall discuss this further later in the book.

As quickly as renewal spread around the country, so did these kinds of horror stories, taking on almost canonical significance in people's minds. The second-hand market flourished: for everyone who had had such a Bad Experience there were dozens who heard about them and reported them as if true, but with no direct knowledge of them themselves. In time a huge mythology flourished, which could be used by the opponents of renewal to prove conclusively how evil it all was.

Today, in spite of the phenomenal growth of charismatic renewal, the same divisions are still present among honest and sincere Christians. Some are for it, many are decidedly not, and to be honest it is sometimes possible to see clearly why they are not. And of course a third group find themselves as confused as I was thirty years ago, unsure about the doctrine and turned off by the practices, but nevertheless with a questing in their hearts which simply will not go away.

My purpose

The reason for my writing this book is to address all three groups of people. In spite of all the difficulties I still believe that charismatic renewal, far from being a strange and aberrant heresy, is nothing more nor less than authentic, mainstream New Testament Christianity. Neither is renewal an option for those who like that sort of thing; it's a central and basic element in Christian living which we can ignore no more than we can ignore other aspects of our faith such as the cross, prayer or forgiveness. When we accept Christ and step into his kingdom, the Spirit comes as part of the package. Being charismatic is not an option, it's a command! Yet so often we regard the work of the Spirit as at best something which need not concern us, and at worst a satanically inspired sideline from the true faith. In a nutshell, I believe that all Christians should be charismatics, and if they're not then they should be!

I hope, first, that this book will be of some use to convince charismatics who may not have had the opportunity to think through their spirituality to any depth. Because renewal is by nature so very experiential, it can be a great temptation to think that theology doesn't really matter. Nothing could be further from the truth, and as I have used some of this material in speaking to groups of fully signed-up charismatics I have been told again and again how useful it is to hear some clear thinking about renewal, and some biblical explanation of their charismatic experiences. I hope some of what I have written will have this *teaching* role.

Second, I have written with those in mind who are out and out opponents of renewal. This means that the book will have an *apologetic* role, which doesn't mean that I'm sorry I wrote it (although I may yet turn out to be) but that it is meant to be a rigorous defence of renewal in the face of disagreement and even hostility. Those who are unhappy with all things charismatic take that position, in my experience, for one of two reasons. For some, the head rules. They simply cannot find this stuff in scripture, and remain unconvinced that what God really wants his church to be doing is behaving charismatically (whatever that is). Others, however, are driven more by their hearts: much as they might find the theology positive, they simply cannot be doing with all this weird exhibitionist behaviour. People are unhappy with renewal from either an intellectual or an emotional point of view. Sometimes both go together, although one or the other usually takes pre-eminence.

I have really tried hard, in writing this book, to listen to those who oppose me and the renewal I stand for, and I have worked hard not to caricature their position but to take it seriously. With those intellectually opposed I will seek to argue logically and biblically, and I have already pointed out to those emotionally opposed that I have a great deal in common with them! But I do want to say two things about the need for honesty in this debate before battle commences. I will try as hard as I can from my side, but we will get nowhere if those to whom I am writing don't play on the same level field.

So one point is to be honest about your objections. Over the years, I have on many occasions entered into debate with those opposed to renewal, and I have found it impossible to hold an intelligent conversation with those who use theological objections as a mask for the real issues, which are emotional. If you think the Bible doesn't sanction renewal, then that's fine, we can work with that. But please don't quote irrelevant Bible verses out of context when the real issue is that the whole thing scares you silly! To be honest enough to admit that you don't much mind what the Bible says about it as long as you never have to come within a million miles of it personally is at least an honest starting point. Sadly, I have not always found people willing to be that honest, and to move on from there is very difficult if people are simply kidding themselves.

My other point in appealing for honesty regards the kind of evidence we bring to bear on our discussions. As I minister as an apologist for renewal, I sometimes encounter arguments against me, which need to be taken seriously, and real pain, which I need to listen to lovingly. But I also hear many arguments against which I want simply to say 'Come off it!' I am not impressed by second- or third-hand stories of someone your auntie's hairdresser's friend's nephew once heard of who had a nervous breakdown after going on an Alpha course, which therefore proves that all renewal is satanic. I am not impressed by the inaccurate use of quasi-psychological terms like 'mass hysteria' or 'hypnotism' by those who have no idea what the terms really mean but who have picked them up from the Sunday colour supplements. And I am not impressed by general quotations of 'lots' of people who have been terminally damaged by renewal. Tell me how many, and tell me some circumstances, and we can talk about that. I might even have no response but to apologize deeply for the misuse of the good gifts of the Holy Spirit which has caused such hurt. But please don't batter me with vagueness: I learnt pretty quickly as a vicar and chairman of church councils that comments such as 'People are saying they're unhappy with such-and-such a development in the life of the church' can be easily disarmed with the question 'How many people?' I've learnt not to listen too seriously to talk like that.

So I hope you will examine my arguments carefully and assess your own hesitations with the same care. Genuine objections I will attempt to take seriously: silly ones, second-hand horror stories, loony fringe caricaturing or sheer fantasies need identifying as such and ignoring. I've had to be very honest and vulnerable to write a book like this; I hope you can be just as honest and vulnerable in reading it. You may not agree with me at the end of the day, but at least you'll have thought it through. And if we are going to have a fight, let's make it a clean fight. You will get upset and annoyed if you feel that I have used inadmissible evidence or that I am being inaccurate in my portrayal of your dearly held views: well, so would I if I heard you doing the same back to me. Let this debate be honest and open, or it will simply be a waste of everyone's time.

Third, I want to address those who are, quite simply, confused about renewal. My aim here is to be as honest as I can, and I hope you won't feel defensiveness coming through in those parts where I do need to take on my opponents more directly and vigorously. Many people will be reading this book because God has been at work in them, stirring them up, raising questions for them, creating discontent with their spiritual status quo. As I know from my own experience, this can be a highly uncomfortable phase to live through, and my prayer is that this book will continue to bring discomfort but will lead people on eventually to the Comforter himself. So if I spend some time refuting an argument which is irrelevant to you, skip a bit and move on. That is allowed!

Our way forward

So how do I intend to attempt to convince you of my thesis, that everyone ought to be charismatic? This book falls into four parts, the logic of which flows (I hope!) inexorably forward. It's important you know where I'm coming from, so in the next chapter I'll be telling you my story. Then in Part I I'll set the scene and explain what I think today's problem is, and why I think that we have this particular problem at this particular time. Next I'll move on to ask what charismatic renewal actually is, so that we all know exactly what we're talking about. Most of us have some kind of a view, but it might well be a bit of a caricature, if we're honest, so we'll need to take a slightly deeper look and see what it's really all about. That will also involve us in a bit of a history lesson too, in order that we understand where this apparently rather new movement has come from.

In Part II I'll set out several reasons why I think it is imperative for us to take renewal seriously, and especially why it is good for us personally. I will endeavour to prove that charismatic renewal should be given the central status for which I'm arguing, by marshalling evidence from several different places in order to convince you of my thesis. The third part will take seriously some of the objections commonly brought against renewal, both emotional and intellectual. Then in Part IV I'll show what a difference renewal can make in some practical, real situations. And finally, in the Epilogue I'll round the book off with an opportunity for some kind of personal response for those who have become convinced along the way.

This book will need to be theological, but I'm aware what a negative word 'theology' is, so I'll try to keep it simple and easy to read and understand. But above all I hope that God will speak through my words: I'm far less interested in convincing people's minds than I am in allowing God to touch their hearts.

Before moving on, let me say something about the word 'renewal'. It's a word which is bandied about quite frequently nowadays, and which is used in quite a few different ways. I need to explain how I'll be using it, and why I've limited it to one particular meaning.

A book called *The Way of Renewal* was published in 1998, edited by my friend and predecessor at Anglican Renewal Ministries, Michael Mitton.[1] It is a collection of stories of different people's experiences of renewal, including a chapter I contributed on my charismatic experience. It is an interesting book, not least because in its range of different stories it raises a very big question about what we mean by the term 'renewal'. Let me explain by looking at two extremes. On the one hand, there are some who might want to say that renewal equals charismatic renewal. The only way that God is acting in the church, the only renewing work in which the Holy Spirit is engaged, is through the charismatics. Nothing else really deserves the name 'renewal'. Most of us, I guess, would say that this is arrogant nonsense: the Holy Spirit is at work in a whole variety of ways, of which charismatic renewal is but one example. I'd certainly hold that view myself.

But the other extreme is to say that anything nice that happens is renewal: we've mended the light switch in the Gents – hallelujah, renewal has come! The word gets so watered-down that it becomes almost meaningless. My own position on the spectrum between these two extremes – and yours as well, I expect – is somewhere between the two. Of course, there is much going on in the church through which the Holy Spirit is at work and which is worthy of the title, without it getting centred on the gift of tongues or any of that stuff. However, and I make no apologies for it, this book is about charismatic renewal and not really about anything else. I'll explain why I think this area is so important in the next couple of chapters – after all, I am paid to promote charismatic renewal, but I wouldn't want you to think that I don't value or thank God for other renewing works of his Holy Spirit.

A genuine work of God?

So why and how should you read this book? Why? Quite simply because it might be right. I cannot think of one move of the Spirit of God which has not been opposed by some of his honest committed followers, leaving others dazed and confused. The Old Testament prophets saw it as they called the nation back to God. Jesus himself taught it about his own ministry into a faith-community desperately in need of renewal, Judaism. He promised it to his disciples as they set about preaching the kingdom of God around the world. You can see it through church history and its revivals, through the Wesleys and their Methodism, and it might just be that we are seeing it today in some of the opponents of charismatic renewal. The fact that people don't like something, of course, doesn't prove it to be a genuine move of God; that's why we have to do some hard thinking and discerning, and that's why people like me have to write apologetics. But echoing through my mind, I have often heard those terrible words of Jesus about the unforgivable sin, as I've been tempted too quickly to pooh-pooh something I've heard about within the church. Jesus issued that warning just after the Pharisees had seen him in action and put it all down to Beelzebub.[2] I have learnt to fear above all else seeing a work of God but not recognizing it as such, and writing it off as a devilish delusion.

Before delving into the nuts and bolts of charismatic renewal, I'd like to share with you my own story of how and why I am where I am today. You may be surprised to hear the confessions of a reluctant charismatic.

Chapter 1
....

Confessions of a Reluctant Charismatic

I can't tell you the exact moment when I became a Christian. I remember at the age of nine signing my name in the 'Decision Book' at church, a book which seemed to come out once a year over the weekend of the Sunday School Anniversary, a memorable weekend because it also tended to coincide with my birthday. I can remember my first real 'spiritual experience' in Aix-en-Provence Cathedral when I was 16, since when I have never doubted the existence of God (apart from one week in 1987, but that's another story).

I could tell you about my statutory year of rebellion when I left home at 18 to read Chemistry and Education at York University, but that wouldn't make very edifying reading. I could also tell you about my second spiritual experience while I was standing in front of a Henry Moore sculpture (a group of people with holes through their middles) on the York campus shortly after I had been slung out of the university for failing some exams. Eventually I returned home, settled into a temporary job in the pharmacy (officially I was a 'sterile technician') of the London (now Royal London) Hospital, and set about reconstructing my abandoned Christian faith.

I remember being in a group Bible study with people from a different church from mine, and listening to a discussion on 'spiritual gifts'. I had not the foggiest idea what they were, or why they needed discussing, but from that day on I couldn't get away from the blessed things. The year was 1971, and charismatic renewal had just broken out in our area, much to the consternation of some of the church leaders.

One evening, while I was praying with a friend, he suddenly told me he had a 'word from the Lord' for me: I was going to become a vicar in the Church of England. This was a strange word to give to a lapsed and struggling Baptist, and I was warned by some wise counsellors not to try to make it happen by my own efforts. Still, I felt that I probably ought at least to begin to find out what the Church of England was all about, since the current view in my circles seemed to be that Anglicans were not real Christians (ecumenism had not made great strides forward in those days). So two different friends invited me to two very different Essex Anglican churches.

On Sunday mornings I was taken to St Laurence's, Upminster, where multitudes of servers minced around the sanctuary, the boss was called 'Father', and you couldn't see the back wall for smoke. And on Tuesday evenings I went to St Paul's, Hainault, where multitudes of bodies lay strewn around the sanctuary, the boss was called Trevor Dearing, and you couldn't see a thing because you had to get there an hour and a half early to get a seat. I hated and feared both churches equally, but I couldn't escape either. Something kept drawing me back week after week to services I knew I would hate. Later on I was to discover that a theologian called Rudolph Otto had identified this phenomenon as the '*mysterium tremendum et fascinans*', the fascinating but terrifying mystery of God which keeps you coming back for more even though you are scared witless in the process.[1]

First steps

The Anglo-Catholic church was relatively easy to understand: the problem was the apostate teaching and practice, but if I only kept my head and clung on to my fundamentalist non-conformist doctrine I would be OK. But it was the charismatic one which really got to me more. I was immediately impressed by a level of New Testament power and authority which I had seen nowhere else. I could see clearly that this looked pretty much like my picture of the early church in action, with heartfelt worship, prayer for healing, demons being expelled, and significant numbers of people finding salvation and moving on into the exercise of supernatural gifts of the Spirit. The only problem was that I was terrified of every second of it! More than anything else I hated the way people raised their hands as they worshipped; I would be the only person in the packed church without my hands in the air because I didn't want to look unusual.

Every week the agenda was the same: after a few songs and the sermon it was 'Who wants to get saved? Come on down!' This was followed by 'Who wants to get baptized in the Spirit?' and then 'Who wants to get healed?' It was the middle bit which was so scary: I was already saved, and I wasn't ill, but what was this Spirit stuff? I watched in terror week after week as people received prayer and the laying on of hands and exploded spontaneously into what I had now discovered was 'speaking in tongues' and/or prophecy, often bursting into tears or flopping to the floor as they did so. The more my head found the preaching convincing, the more my heart dreaded what I had by now realized was that inevitable moment when I would end up down the front behaving in some outrageous way. I fought it successfully for several months until finally God took over and I found myself kneeling at the altar rail with not the slightest recollection of how I had got there.

The vicar and his assistant moved inexorably closer, and my desperate desire to run grew stronger, a bit like the feeling I get in the dentist's waiting room. Should I escape and put it off until another day? Or should I finish what it had taken such effort and heartache to get started? The praying hands reached my neighbour at the rail: she immediately burst out in tongues and, as I sneaked a glance at her, wept with such an expression of total bliss on her face.

And then it was me. I waited in terror as hands were laid on me and prayers were said. Absolutely nothing whatsoever happened. The pray-ers moved on and I got up from the rail and went back to my seat, feeling nothing except profound disappointment. It hadn't worked. That which I greatly feared had not come upon me. Zilch.

Over the next two years friends prayed for me with ever-increasing fervency and an ever-tightening grip on my head. My emotions ran the gamut from 'Is there something wrong with me?' to 'Well, I never really wanted it anyway!' The more people prayed, the more nothing happened. I became better informed, of course, and I now knew most of what there was to know about charismatic renewal. I devoured books on how to be filled with the Spirit, charismatic theology, how to do the gifts of the Spirit and all the rest, but it just would not happen for me.

What exactly was the 'it' which so stubbornly refused to happen? I wasn't sure, but it had to be something more than nothing whatsoever. I suppose I was expecting to burst suddenly into tongues, or to feel the kind of ecstasy I so often saw on the faces of others, but instead life continued as before. Well-meaning friends assured me that I had in fact been baptized in the Spirit, since God-will-always-give-the-Holy-Spirit-to-those-who-ask-him-Luke-eleven-thirteen, but I questioned the cash value of a spiritual experience which had made not a jot of difference to me. Anyway, others seemed to take to being charismatic easily enough; why not me?

'It' finally happened two years later while I was in bed one night in a B & B in what is now called Dyfed but was then Pembrokeshire. I can remember it clearly because the bed had those horrid nylon sheets which got caught in your toenails every time you turned over. Getting up in the morning was like Lazarus trying to get out of his graveclothes – OK, I'm alive, now unbind me! Very hesitantly I began to speak in tongues, and found after a few minutes that it was a doddle. I felt moderately ecstatic, but it was nothing to do with the Spirit: it was sheer relief that at long last I had somehow made the grade, and brought to a close two of the most spiritually miserable years of my life. But the real problems were just beginning.

On the way

By now I had abandoned (for a while at least) my flirtation with Anglo-Catholicism and had been confirmed into the Church of England in a somewhat safer-feeling evangelical church. I was on my way towards a selection conference for ordination, and I was a paid-up head-held-high charismatic. The only problem was that I still hated it all. Most of all I still hated the arms-in-the-air bit. Each week I would go to church and check the hymnboard to see if we were going to be singing anything dangerous. The worst was 'I am the Bread of Life', but there were plenty of others. How I came to love safe traditional hymns! I might have surrendered control of my speech to God, but no way was he getting my arms! Worship became more than ever a nightmare, but now if I was officially 'in' I had somehow not just to endure it but to pretend I was enjoying it.

The first time I ever put my arms in the air was, of all places, in a convent during my ACCM (now called ABM), a residential selection conference at which the fate of a bunch of hopeful Anglican would-be ordinands is decided by a board of selectors. The nuns had heard a small group, led by a candidate who was a charismatic musician, singing some worship songs, and had been so taken with them that they asked the group if they wouldn't mind recording them on to tape. I was roped in – I knew all the songs, after all – and as we joined in the clandestine after-hours recording session I was so moved by the music, and so far from home, that I took the plunge and risked it. The universe, much to my amazement, did not come to an abrupt end, and I was filled with a sense of glorious naughtiness and tremendous relief. On reflection I don't think the position of my arms was anywhere near such a big issue to God as was my refusal to surrender them to him, but from that time on I became free, free to use my body in praise or not, as I wished. The tension vanished, and I was set free to enjoy charismatic worship, something I had not done for years.

In the meantime I'd married Chris, and shortly after that we moved away from that church and joined another, which was even more overtly charismatic. It was here that for the first time we encountered the seriously loony fringe. There were some great people at the church, but the whole thing was so spiritually intense, and seemed to attract so many people who were on the edge of being dotty, that we began to question whether we really wanted to be charismatics if that was how we'd turn out. So when, some years later, as a soon-to-be-ordained deacon, I was interviewed for a curacy, I told my potential boss that I had indeed been through a charismatic phase, but that I had grown out of it and left all that behind. I would happily fit into his somewhat Anglo-Catholic church, I told him, having rediscovered that strand of my spirituality while in training at King's, London. Chris and I had no desire to see the parish developing along the lines we had experienced before.

A year or so in, we had a visit from a friend in the parish who had recently come to faith. She was in some distress, and told us she was being plagued by a series of gruesome nightmares. We duly prayed for her and the nightmares stopped immediately, only to be replaced by something even more scary. She had woken in the night to find herself speaking in a strange language. What on earth was going on, she asked. It felt good – really good, in fact – but what on earth was it? With a rare flash of spiritual insight we realized that we had inadvertently baptized her in the Holy Spirit (or rather we had asked Jesus to) and she had become a charismatic. Others in the parish began experiencing similar things: we could only conclude that God was using them to rekindle in us the charismatic spirituality which we had abandoned. I think it was at that time that I first became a charismatic leader, as I began to teach on renewal and encourage people to experience it for themselves.

A second curacy in a charismatic megachurch followed, and the rest, as they say, is history. I went on to become a proper vicar of my own church, and again we saw charismatic renewal break out in the parish, although of course with such good, balanced leadership that there was nothing remotely like a loony fringe! As my love for and understanding of renewal grew, so did my love for the C of E, to which I felt God had specifically called me. When a visiting Vineyard pastor from America prophesied over me that God wanted to use me for the renewing of the Church of England, I understood that to mean 'You're doing a good job, mate, even though you're an Anglican: keep it up!' But when three months later I was invited to apply for the job at Anglican Renewal Ministries, his words flashed back to me. That's what I now do, and I am totally committed to both Anglicanism and charismatic renewal, notwithstanding the funny bits of both. I don't believe for one moment that God has given up on the historic denominations, and my calling is to work for the letting loose of the Holy Spirit in one of them.

Where I'm coming from

Why have I told you all this? Because it's really important that you understand just what a reluctant charismatic I was. I'm going to try to convince you in this book that you need to be a charismatic too, if you're not one already, so you need to know that I am not an uncritical fanatic of the movement or its culture. My journey into renewal was slow, painful and hesitant. I still balk at some of its excesses, and I still find much of it embarrassing. I really do understand those who have been turned off renewal because of other charismatics they have seen in action. I know charismatics can be triumphalist, unthinking, emotionally unbalanced, naïve, and all the other adjectives they get thrown at them. But nevertheless I am more than ever convinced in my head that charismatic spirituality is something the church desperately needs: the problems do not invalidate the core spirituality. It's an old adage, but the answer to misuse really is right use rather than disuse.

I am also totally committed to the *renewal* of the church, and not to some kind of attempt to throw it all away and start again. As a parish priest, my crusade was to lead a church into renewal as fully as possible but also as thoughtfully and sensibly as possible, while staying fully committed to the denomination I belonged to, and this mission continues in my current job. This book is an extension of that mission, and I hope that God might use it towards the renewing of more Christians and more of his church.

Part One

Introducing Charismatic Renewal

Chapter 2

Take Your Pick!

When I was young we didn't own a telly, so I used to look forward to our weekly trips to my Nan and Granddad's in Dagenham every Friday after school. As well as sausages and chips and ring dough-nuts (called 'Dunkies' – remember them?) for tea, I loved watching my favourite TV programme (in fact my only TV programme) *Take Your Pick*. Michael Miles, the host, would employ various tactics to use the contestants to entertain the audience (I love that later Monty Python phrase 'ritual humiliation of the fat and stupid'), after which they could choose a key to a particular box which might contain tonight's star prize, or possibly a worthless booby prize. As we huddled round the 9-inch screen each week, screech-ing 'Open the box!' or, less frequently 'Take the money!' we little realized that what we were watching was to become an icon of a later worldview.

A few 'isms'

The word 'postmodernism' is one which is used often nowadays, and the concept it describes is indeed an important one, not least for our purposes in this book. I won't go into it in great detail, but we do need to look at it a bit in order to understand why the things I'm saying in this book need saying.

We all live within a particular culture, and the culture we live in tells us the things which are self-evidently true about life, the universe and everything. This great overarching story is called a 'metanarrative'. But it is a historical fact that once every few hundred years cultures die, and what was obvious before is no longer obvious at all. People quite simply stop believing the metanarrative.

The last major cultural shift in the West took place in the seventeenth century. Before that, Britain based its culture on Christianity. The metanarrative told us that we lived in a world created by a God who cared for it and sustained it, and who could be known and related to by humans. This metanarrative was known as Theism, and it wasn't so much that people learned this story – rather, they imbibed it with their mothers' milk. It was just, well, obvious. Now of course, not everyone did know this God or relate to him, but that didn't invalidate the story: those who rejected Christianity at least knew what they were rejecting.

But with the rise of experimental science in the seventeenth century, people began to feel that they needed an omnipotent God a lot less than they had done before. The more we understood the universe and the way it worked, the less we needed God to explain it for us. Branches of science like astronomy, for example, made it increasingly clear that the universe worked according to a set of rules: the task of science was to discover all it could about those rules. And of course, the more we understood, the more we could control: by tweaking the rules a little bit we could do all manner of things which had previously been down to God alone. A God who healed illnesses, for example, gave way to doctors who could do the same. The Christian culture, with its understanding of a God who could and might intervene in the smooth running of the world, shuddered and died, to be replaced by a new culture which came to be called 'modernism', and a metanarrative which said that mankind controlled the universe, or at least we could do if we kept on making new discoveries and getting better and better at science. Since science now ruled, the things which science could not investigate, like God, the supernatural, faith, and so on, were relegated to the realm of 'superstition': only that which could be put, as it were, under the microscope, was thought to be real and valid. Many people did, of course, still have a Christian faith, but it was increasingly separated from the 'real' material world of which science was telling us more and more. And even faith became the prey of the scientists: work on the 'psychology of religion' became popular as scientists sought to understand this strange phenomenon called 'faith' much as they might investigate a rare animal or an unexpected volcanic eruption.

This cultural shift didn't happen overnight, of course. When philosophers told us finally that God had died, it had been a slow, lingering death, not a sudden seizure. There was a short bridge period when people couldn't quite bring themselves to dispense with God altogether. Theism was gradually replaced by Deism, the belief that although God had been responsible for the creation of the universe, he had no further interest in it now. The picture often used was that of a clockmaker, who with infinite skill had made a wonderful machine, wound it up and set it going, and then had put it on the shelf and gone away to get on with something else. As such, the Creator was someone to be admired and respected, but not loved, worshipped or served.

Soon Deism gave way, with inexorable logic, to Modernism, although it is worth saying that it is actually alive and well today in pockets of the world such as the Scouting movement, Freemasonry and the Anglican 'Eight O'Clock Communion' congregations who want to do their 'duty' to 'the Almighty' without really believing that he wants to be involved in any tangible way in their day-to-day lives.

So for the past couple of hundred years we in the West have lived with a story which tells us that science is, in effect, God. In a sermon I once asked people to raise their hands if they believed that one day we would find a cure for AIDS. About half the congregation put their hands up: I then accused them of believing in Scientism, the belief that science was omnipotent.[1] As well as this lie, Modernism also tells us that the only 'real' things in life are things we can feel, see, hear, taste or smell, and the only way to true peace and fulfilment is through buying and owning things. It is the Argos catalogue, not the Bible, which rules in most people's minds today.

But during the last few decades this metanarrative has in turn begun to creak and groan, and is currently in its final death-agonies. People have begun to see through the lie of Modernism:

the other half of my congregation, who didn't put their hands up because they had no faith that all our problems *could* be solved given enough time, effort and scientific research, also represented a significant area of belief in society at large. Many have seen the other side of the very real benefits of science: we can now control or even eradicate many diseases which would once have wiped out entire populations, but we have also created the means to destroy the earth: the pill has made birth control much more simple and convenient, but it has affected the morality of a generation and given rise to an unprecedented number of casualties in terms of sexually transmitted diseases, people scarred through lack of depth and relationship in their sexual encounters, and, paradoxically, unwanted pregnancies and abortions. The optimism of a culture in which humankind was believed to be evolving gradually towards perfection has been replaced by a cynicism born of the slaughter of two world wars, the corruption of politicians and others in author-ity, our total failure to use scientific means to deal effectively with problems of famine and starvation, and the clear sense that things are getting daily worse, not better. Not that long ago, UN aircraft were dropping bombs on Kosovo while thousands of refugees were starving and dying on the borders of neighbouring countries: this scene seems to provide a perfect icon for the failure of science to deliver the goods it promised.

There is also an increasing sense that material things do not pro-vide all the answers, and more and more people are on a quest for some kind of 'spirituality' or contact with something which is clearly beyond the reach of science. Many people in America have a therapist in the way Brits have a dentist, and the rise of the influ-ence of horoscopes, 'alternative' therapies, occultism and the like demonstrates that there is a longing in our hearts which needs something more than the Argos catalogue for its fulfilment. Mod-ernism is in terminal decline, and the materialistic metanarrative is no longer believed. Since we don't know where we're going, we have to define ourselves by where we've been: we live in a time after modernism has passed away, so academics are calling us 'postmodernists'. This is probably, like Deism a couple of hundred years earlier, a bridge period on the way to a whole new culture, but we'll have to wait and see both what it turns out to be like and what academics will call it.

The 'Pick'n'Mix' culture

Now for reasons which we need not go into, one of the characteristics of Postmodernity is what has been called 'Pick'n'Mix'. You know those sweet counters in Woolies? We always visit them when we're going on holiday: we have many hours of driving ahead of us so we need something to suck on the way. We grab a little bag and set about making some choices: I like Murray Mints and rum toffees, so a few of them go into the bag. Chris likes Chocolate Eclairs, the boys like Coca-Cola-flavoured worms, Vicki likes Starbursts, so in they go. None of us, however, is keen on Butter Brazils, and chocolate things melt in the hot French sun so we miss them out. Finally the selection is complete, and we go to the till to find we've spent over £8 on tooth decay.

Postmodernism is a Pick'n'Mix culture in that everything is up for grabs. You literally take your pick from a wide variety of choices, and it's the luck of the draw whether you win or lose. No-one else is to blame; you did the choosing, and so you must take the consequences, whether a week for two in the Caribbean or a booby-prize like a bent wire coathanger. What's more, our choices are up for grabs as a matter of free personal selection. Like all cultures postmodernism has a metanarrative, but this one is different: the metanarrative of postmodernism is that there is no metanarrative, there is no overarching meaning to the universe – it is just up to us to make our own meaning. There is no such thing as 'truth': whatever I want to think is true is true for me. So we take our pick, selecting bits from here, there and everywhere and putting them all together so that we can see how that feels, and whether or not our bag works for us. Postmodern architecture combines all sorts of different styles side by side to create an overall effect which is meant to please, or at least to please the architect. A visit to Canary Wharf in East London will provide a good example of this approach. Postmodern music might place Gregorian chant, a synthesized drum loop, some Celtic whistle and jazz sax together into the same piece, and of course postmodern religion is to be found in what has come to be known as 'New Age', a doctrineless collection of self-help, alternative therapies and occultism from which anyone can Pick-'n'Mix their own belief system.

Optional – or essential?

Well, all that was fascinating, wasn't it, but what on earth has it all got to do with charismatic renewal? Quite simply that this Pick'n'Mix attitude to life has infected the church as well. What does postmodern Christianity look like? Well, you might choose to be into Celtic spirituality, or you might go for Taizé instead. You might really fancy Iona worship, or Vineyard, or Dance, Rave, Trance or Jungle might be more your scene. You might have been seriously zapped by Toronto, or you might prefer quieter contemplative prayer. You might like incense, or you might not. You might be into pilgrimage, or Messianic Judaism; so the list goes on, and basically whatever you get off on, that's OK for you. You simply take your pick.

Now that of itself may not be a major problem: it is what life is like at the moment, and we can no more opt out of it than a fish can opt out of the water it swims in. After all, God has made us all different, and we do have different tastes and personal styles. I don't believe my predilection for Berlioz and reggae is a matter of that much concern to God. But it can be a problem if in my picking and mixing I choose to leave behind some central areas of Christian discipleship, which I see merely as options for those who like that kind of thing. 'I don't do prayer' is, most would agree, simply not an acceptable option for the follower of Jesus. This is no doubt happening with many areas of Christian truth, such as 'I don't do celibacy' or 'Tithing isn't my thing' or 'I don't want to be tied down to one church or denomination.' But I believe that one particularly dangerous manifestation of this attitude is the way in which Christians feel that it is perfectly permissible to disobey the Bible's exhortations to 'be filled with the Spirit' and to 'desire earnestly the gifts of the Spirit'. If people want to go charismatic, the rhetoric goes, that is up to them. If it works for them, that's OK, but it isn't my thing. What goes on in private between consenting adults is fine for them, and of course we must all be tolerant (the highest virtue of all in a postmodern world) but don't bring any of that charismatic stuff too near me. I want to suggest in this book that this attitude is not only destructive of personal discipleship, but has damaged the church beyond measure. To be charismatic, I want to suggest, is not something for those who happen to get off on it, but is authentic, mainstream New Testament Christianity. To ignore this aspect of our faith is disobedient and dangerous, and should not be a matter for personal choice but a discipleship imperative.

What is this 'charismatic' business I'm trying to sell you? Let's move on to explore that question next.

Chapter 3
· · · · · · · · · · · · · · · · · ·

What Is This Thing Called 'Charismatic'?

I've said that being charismatic is not an option but a command, but that does raise a fundamental question: what does 'being charismatic' mean, and what does it entail? In order to answer that question we need a bit of a history lesson, and we'll need to begin in the world of the Old Testament.

Hints and promises

From time to time God's people might have experiences which are variously described as having the Spirit of God 'come upon' them, being 'filled with the Spirit' and so on. Usually these experiences enabled them to do things which they might otherwise not have been able to do, in such areas as prophetic gifting, leadership or artistry, but such 'anointings' were usually temporary and transient. However, there were hints that it would be within God's purposes to turn what were temporary events into permanent states. The clearest examples of this are to be found in the prophecies of Jeremiah, Ezekiel and Joel. Jeremiah looked forward to a time when God would

'make a new covenant
with the house of Israel
and with the house of Judah.
It will not be like the covenant
I made with their ancestors
when I took them by the hand

to lead them out of Egypt,
because they broke my covenant,
 though I was a husband to them,'
 declares the LORD.
'This is the covenant that I will make with the house of Israel
 after that time,' declares the LORD.
'I will put my law in their minds
 and write it on their hearts.
I will be their God,
 and they will be my people.
No longer will they teach their neighbours,
 or say to one another, "Know the LORD,"
because they will all know me,
 from the least of them to the greatest,'
 declares the LORD.

(Jeremiah 31:31—4)

What had been an external relationship, based on rules and regula-
tions, was to be replaced by a new way of relating to God, which
was internalized and personal. People would instinctively know
what would please God, and would delight to do it. Although the
Holy Spirit is not specifically mentioned in this passage, an equivalent part of Ezekiel's prophecy explains further that God

will give you a new heart and put a new spirit in you; I will remove
from you your heart of stone and give you a heart of flesh. And I will
put my Spirit in you and move you to follow my decrees and be careful to keep my laws.

(Ezekiel 36:26—7)

This new relationship with God, with its instinctive knowledge of
how to live in ways which please him, will come about when he
puts his Spirit not 'on' people but 'in' them. Joel makes this even
more explicit when he prophesies of God's plan in the future to

pour out my Spirit on all people.
Your sons and daughters will prophesy,

> your old men will dream dreams,
> your young men will see visions.
> Even on my servants, both men and women,
> I will pour out my Spirit in those days.
>
> (Joel 2:28—9)

Getting drenched

John the Baptist made the radical announcement that this prophecy was about to be fulfilled when he proclaimed Jesus as the one who would 'baptize' people in the Holy Spirit (Mark 1:8). The word which we translate as 'baptize' had the meaning of immersing and drenching something: when I wash my car (all too rarely, I'm afraid to say) I begin by 'baptizing' my sponge in soapy water. The sponge goes into the water, but also the water goes into the sponge. 'John the Drencher' would not be an inaccurate translation of John's title. Jesus was similarly to be the baptizer or drencher in the Holy Spirit, but although the Spirit was clearly at work in his own ministry and that of his disciples, the promise was still unfulfilled by the time he died. However, some of his parting words to his friends were that they should wait in Jerusalem because the promise was about to be fulfilled and power from on high was soon to clothe them (Luke 24:49).

Ten days later, on the Jewish festival of Pentecost, the Spirit came upon the waiting disciples in an explosion of wind and fire, thrusting them out into the street in praise and witness. The drenching had happened, and what a drenching it was! It was marked by outbursts of praise and the gift of tongues, which we will discuss later, but which for now may be defined as the ability to praise or pray to God in a language which you've never learnt and which you don't understand. Such was the riotous behaviour of the apostles that they were accused of hitting the bottle. Peter, their spokesman on that occasion, explained what had happened by quoting Joel's words, and he called on all who wanted to follow Christ from then on to turn from the sin of lives lived for themselves, commit themselves to a life of faith, and to show that they had done so by being baptized in water as the initiation ceremony into the body which was later to be called the church. As a result, they too could experience this same gift of the Holy Spirit, as could their descendants after them.

As the church thrived and grew, it became a company of people treated with awe because of the supernatural power which was so evidently displayed. The sick were healed, demonized people were set free, and stories of miracles abounded. Speaking in tongues, as the apostles had on the day of Pentecost, was commonplace. But as time went on, and as the church grew in numbers, in influence and therefore in its need for structures and organization, the power of the Spirit was less in evidence. Within a couple of centuries a fringe movement grew up, founded by one Montanus, whose followers experienced supernatural gifts of the Holy Spirit. Our accounts of this group show that they may have been a bit over the top, but the response of the Christian 'establishment' is interesting: Montanists were denounced as heretics and hounded from the church. Clearly some of the more extreme aspects of the Spirit's work had ceased in the mainstream church, such that those who experienced them were seen as beyond the pale. This was not a good thing which had gone a bit wild and needed careful correction: rather, it was something which needed removing decisively from the life of the church.

These supernatural aspects of the Spirit's gifting to the church never entirely stopped, but they do seem to have lessened in their frequency at different phases of the church's history. John Wimber traces throughout church history different records of people being involved in healing, prophetic gifts, deliverance ministry and speaking in tongues, but his conclusion was that the frequency of such gifts was patchy: when the leadership of the church endorsed them, they abounded, but when the leadership was set against them, they all but disappeared.[1]

The charismatic movement

However, a major new outpouring of the Spirit occurred around the turn of the twentieth century. Isolated individuals around the world had begun to experience tongues and other gifts, but in 1900 in Topeka, Kansas, the Spirit was poured out in power on a group of farmers who were studying the book of Acts in a barn. At around the same time, at a church in Los Angeles, there was a mighty outpouring of the Spirit which resulted in people in their thousands flocking from around the world to see what was going on and to take the blessing back home with them. Since what was happening appeared to be the same as what had happened on the day of Pentecost, a new denomination, called the Pentecostal church, was born. This denomination thrived and grew, and in spite of some internal splits over finer points of doctrine it continued to grow in numbers and in influence around the world. As people came into an experience of 'baptism in the Spirit' they usually left whatever church they had come from and became Pentecostals.

But in 1960 an American Anglican priest was baptized in the Spirit, and took the radical step of staying within the Episcopalian (or Anglican) church. The 'charismatic movement', which had been gestating quietly in several isolated pockets around the country, was born, and began to grow world-wide as more and more people realized that they could live out their new charismatic spirituality within their existing denominations. Charismatic Anglicans, Baptists, Methodists, Catholics and others held on to the ethos and traditions of their churches, and began to influence those churches with 'renewal'. Spiritual gifts such as tongues, prophecy and healings began to be a part of traditional mainstream churches' worship, and such churches were often revitalized and began to grow. New styles of music came to the fore, and charismatic doctrines began to be formed which differed in some degree from those of the Pentecostal denominations. In particular, Pentecostal emphasis on a 'Second Blessing', a baptism in the Spirit as a second and subsequent event to conversion, was replaced by the belief that conversion and baptism were meant to convey the fullness of the Spirit without any subsequent events, and the emphasis on the gift of tongues as a necessary proof of genuine conversion was replaced with the understanding of tongues as one gift among many, given at the will of the Spirit.

We have reached the point today where charismatic renewal is widely recognized within the church as a valid spirituality, and where the charismatic and Pentecostal movements between them were predicted, by the end of the second millennium, to account for over 600 million of the world's Christians – no mean feat for a movement only a hundred or so years old.[2] Virtually every Christian denomination has been touched by renewal, and it has brought new life and vitality; large and growing churches world-wide are statistically very likely indeed to be charismatic churches.

Yet, as I have explained, charismatic renewal has not gained universal acceptance, and is now often viewed in churches as one option among many in choosing one's spirituality.

Being charismatic

But what does 'being charismatic' entail? What does it look like? Here we immediately have a problem, since people do not 'go charismatic' in a vacuum. An individual and personal experience of the Spirit is the initiation into a corporate church culture which might look very different in different places. The renewing power of the Spirit is just that: power to renew something which already exists, rather than to start from scratch with something brand new. Pentecostalism became a denomination because it created a specific culture: charismatic renewal remains a 'movement' because it will look very different as it puts on the clothes of different denominations and churchmanships.

Take a lemon, for example. You won't have to be much of a botanist to recognize it as a citrus fruit, along with oranges, grapefruits, tangerines, clementines and that ever-increasing number of species of other little orange jobbies which I can never tell apart. A proper botanist would be able to tell you exactly what defines 'citrusness', but we mere mortals can get some way along the road: all the members of the group share a thick skin which you can't eat, with white pith underneath, then little segments of juicy bits each surrounded by a skin or membrane. The more astute of us would probably know that a parsnip isn't a citrus fruit. But we would also fairly easily be able to tell the difference between different citrus fruits (apart from the little orange jobbies). Most of us would not by mistake eat a lemon for breakfast or squeeze grapefruit juice on to our prawn cocktail.

It's just the same with charismatics; you wouldn't squeeze them on to your prawn cocktail either. They all recognizably share a common characteristic, which is an experience of baptism in the Spirit and the use of supernatural gifts of the Spirit, but the way in which that spirituality is expressed can vary tremendously. I recently spent a week at an Anglo-Catholic renewal conference: there were the same tongues, worship songs, times of prayer ministry and so on that I had often experienced in Vineyard churches, but there were also vestments, candles, holy water and clouds of smoke! Last summer I went to a festival called New Wine, where the exercise of charismatic spirituality was totally non-liturgical and Vineyardy in style: a month later, at our Anglican Renewal Ministries conference, we worshipped together from a book using the richness of the Anglican liturgical tradition, but saw exactly the same manifestations of the Spirit's presence. Methodists 'do' renewal in a Methodist way, New Churches do it their way. At the risk of sounding like a set of car-stickers, Baptists do it under water, Roman Catholics do it with candles, Evangelicals do it on the Word, and Anglicans like me often do it in the middle of the road!

This is important to grasp, because some people reading this book may be doing so out of an antithesis to renewal. However, in feeling that renewal isn't something they would like to be a part of, they may be reacting primarily against a particular culture in which they have seen it expressed and which feels alien to them. This raises the question 'Do we have to buy the whole package, or is there a core spirituality which we can keep even if we choose to discard the wrapping and dress it up in our own church culture?' I'll return to this question in due course, but for now let me say simply that the answer to that second part of the question is a resounding 'Yes'. It is already dressed up in a huge variety of cultures, and if you don't like what you have seen so far it may be that your aversion to the wrapping paper has made you reject a valuable gift.

So what at base level is charismatic renewal? It is rooted in an initial experience called 'baptism in the Spirit', of which more later, but it is not just about a one-off experience; the experience leads to a whole new lifestyle, and a whole new way of relating to God. In other words, it is a 'spirituality', and to an exploration of that spirituality we must now turn.

Chapter 4
....

Charismatic Spirituality

One of the things I love to do when I'm out speaking is to ask people to brainstorm the kind of words which come to mind when they hear talk of 'charismatic renewal'. The responses I get are interesting: they often major on things like 'happy-clappy', 'hands in the air', 'bodies on the floor', 'guitars', 'mindless' or 'unthinking', and 'triumphalism'. Charismatic renewal clearly does have an image, and there does seem to be inherent in these responses the idea that charismatics are on to something, something recognizable, different and slightly weird.

We might be forgiven for feeling, then, that if this is what renewal is really all about, we'll happily leave it to someone else to be renewed! Is that it? Is renewal nothing more than a set of musical instruments, physical movements and mental attitudes, or is there more to it than that?

Perhaps a more objective assessment of renewal spirituality can be gained from those looking in on it from outside. Kilian McDonnell, an American Roman Catholic and commentator on things charismatic, set about collecting such material. Many denominations, and provinces within denominations, who found themselves affected by renewal commissioned official reports on it. The Church of England did so in 1980, and many other churches have produced similar documents. McDonnell collected these together in a massive three-volume work which he entitled, significantly, *Presence, Power and Praise*.[1] I can think of no better headings under which to describe what I consider to be the core of charismatic spirituality, although I shall want to add two more 'P's to his three.

Presence

Virtually every one of the documents in McDonnell's collection singles out the *presence* of God as a key factor in renewal spirituality. Bishop Colin Buchanan, who edited the official Church of England report, says that:

> To worship is to meet God.
>   For the charismatics, worship is meeting, and the Lord is present with them in power ... This is a great undergirding factor in everything else we have to discuss.[2]

Old Testament scholar John Goldingay similarly asserts that

> Charismatic spirituality assumes that it is normal on a continuing basis for the church and for the individual believer to have a felt sense of the presence and power of God, and a felt joy in God or enthusiasm for God.[3]

For charismatics, and particularly for charismatics at worship, the presence of God is not just a theological truth, but also a personal experiential reality.

But surely God is always present everywhere? How can we talk about his presence as though there were the possibility of his absence? In my *Living Liturgy* I discuss this question,[4] differentiating not between presence and absence but between different types of presence. Charismatic spirituality does not require us to believe that at some times God is around and at others he is not. Rather, it is about the intensity with which we can become aware of his presence, and our relationship with the present God. Most Christians believe that in some sense God is there with them: charismatics would want to ask what the cash value of that presence is. To worship a God whom we expect to meet with in some kind of a life-changing encounter, a God who might *do* something, who might make a difference in some tangible way, is a major charismatic emphasis. The charismatic comes to prayer or worship with a high degree of expectancy, and will often go away changed in some way as a result.

I'm not trying to say, of course, that for those who wouldn't call themselves charismatics none of this is true; but I do believe that this kind of expectancy of an encounter with God is a distinctive of charismatic spirituality not found universally across the church!

Power

My second 'P' stands for power, the belief in a nutshell that the God who is present with us is a God who does stuff. Let me illustrate this with a piece of Anglican liturgy. In the prayers of intercession during the Communion Service in the now passed away *Alternative Service Book* (this text is still available as an option in the new *Common Worship* Order One Communion Service) we quite rightly prayed for those who were sick or suffering. But listen to how we prayed for them: 'Give them courage and hope in their difficulties, and bring them the joy of your salvation.'

In other words, help them to feel better about being ill! There is little apparent expectation expressed in that prayer that God will intervene in a sovereign way to make a difference; indeed, it was an unwritten doctrine of the church during the modernist age that 'of course we can't believe in an interventionist God, who pops in and out of human history whimsically changing things'. If you believe that God created the universe with a set of inbuilt laws to keep it going, like some vast machine, of course it would mess things up if he kept fiddling with the mechanisms.

But fewer and fewer people see the world like that any more. Even many scientists are now seeing the universe as being much more random than they had previously thought, and the solid dividing wall between science and faith is crumbling fast. But it is where this outdated worldview still holds sway that charismatics come into the most direct confrontation to its dogmas. Of course, many Anglicans do believe in healing, and other parts of the liturgy are more expectant than the line I quoted above, but this prayer, which was prayed by thousands around the country on a weekly basis for a period of twenty years, seems to me both to describe exactly this belief in a God of limited power and also to a high degree to cause it! A whole theology of healing has grown up in the church to explain the fact that no-one actually expects anyone to get better. You know the sort of thing: 'we'll all get healed one day when we die', or the dismissal of mere 'curing' of illnesses such as Jesus used to do as though that were something altogether too substandard to mention. Rather, we should aim for 'healing' or 'wholeness', which is that we have well-rounded personalities even though we may still be as ill as ever. How anyone can claim to be whole while still being ill is a mystery to me: to be whole shouldn't you be sorted out emotionally *and* physically well? This kind of un-biblical double-thinking is the practical expression of a theology of a powerless God, or at least of a God who is relatively powerless. Charismatics, by contrast, believe in a God who, like the Jesus who walked our earth, will intervene to work miracles, and the fact that miracles are perhaps seen more rarely than they would like does nothing to daunt them from believing in the possibility of healing and hoping and praying for it to happen. Philosophical arguments about the impossibility of an interventionist God cut no ice at all: their Bibles very clearly tell stories about a God who is intimately involved in human history, and who can even make the sun stay still or change direction if he so chooses. Not only that; their own personal experience is that God already has intervened, to baptize them in his Holy Spirit and to work miracles in answer to their prayers. So charismatic spirituality is a spirituality of the power of God, power to make a real tangible difference. As Colin Urquhart said of his early experience in a church moving into renewal, 'Something new was needed: we need to stop praying for the sick and start healing them!'[5]

An important subset of the belief in a God of power is, of course, the belief in his power imparted to us by the gift of the Holy Spirit. Jesus tells his followers in Acts 1:8 that when the Spirit comes upon them they will receive power, and Paul explains in some of his letters what that power might entail. In 1 Corinthians 12 he lists nine supernatural gifts of the Holy Spirit, and it is the expectation

28

of the charismatic today that these powerful tools for service will be a part of his or her daily experience. More, it is one of the defining marks of charismatic renewal that these supernatural abilities are very much alive and available to the church today.

In fact, the word 'supernatural' is misleading: for the charismatic it is not that normal church is natural and that renewal has somehow lifted things on to a new, supernatural plane. Normal church, where the power of the Spirit is not fully in evidence and where outdated modernist mindsets persist, is subnatural: it is an encounter with and an openness to the Spirit which makes it naturally what God always intended it to be.

Praise

Most people, in trying to define charismatic renewal, would almost certainly say something about worship. It is in worship that charismatic spirituality is most publicly 'on show'. Charismatics are renowned for their exuberance in worship, and their music often focuses on intimacy with God, addressing him face to face in the first person, where traditional hymns are more often sung *about* him rather than *to* him.[6] One liturgist wrote that in the past in the Church of England we have tended to regard praise in worship as 'unmanly and unnecessary', since God is a well-bred Englishman who would find our praise as embarrassing to receive as we would to give. Renewal, however, has changed all that, at least in the liturgical scene. Charismatics are not afraid to praise God, and are not ashamed to be seen doing it.

This fact follows on, of course, from my first heading. If our God is a somewhat remote or distant figure, one whom we respect from afar, or if he is someone whom we learnt about forty or more years ago in Sunday School but whom we have never met personally, it is understandable that we might get just a tiny bit less excited about him than if we met him only yesterday, and know we met him because we were healed by that encounter or touched powerfully by him in some other way. Exuberant praise is the outflow of a genuine experience of the presence of God, and the lack of it in many of our churches might be a sign of the unreality of God's presence with us.

So how do charismatics praise? By giving it all they've got! Most notable is the use of their bodies: the biblical idea of 'lifting holy hands' to God in worship is taken literally, and the *really* liberated might even dance, kneel, lie flat on the floor, or do other outrageous things with their bodies. 'Liberated' seems to be the key word here: most churches will expect worshippers to use their bodies in some way during the service, by standing to sing, kneeling to pray, crossing themselves, genuflecting or whatever, but usually only in a pretty formalized way, and usually when they are told to by whoever is at the front or at particular set points in the service. Charismatic praise is about the freedom to express your love to God using your physical being as you want to at any given moment, and although there is obviously a certain amount of 'liturgy' built in, there is seldom, in my experience, any pressure to conform, contrary to the fantasies of terrified non-charismatics who have been caught up in a session of renewed worship by mistake!

Perhaps the other most significant ingredient in charismatic worship is its music. It is an historical fact that every new move of God down the centuries has been accompanied by a new outpouring of hymnody. Even from the time of the Psalms the cry comes down to us again and again to sing a new song to God: in every case our praise to God is as a result of him having done something, and it seems to be that when he does something of national or even international significance the response he calls out from our hearts is new music.

Charismatic renewal is no exception to this, and since the early seventies there has been a steady flow of new music coming from the charismatic world. My *Hymns and Spiritual Songs* discusses this current manifestation of the 'new song' in some detail, but the basic characteristics are of music in a contemporary style (or rather a seventies style, if we're honest, which is at least slightly more contemporary than Isaac Watts or A.M. Toplady), with intimate lyrics usually addressed to God rather than to others about God. The charismatic music scene is a huge industry world-wide; songs from this stable are regularly used in churches and cathedrals around the country, and are constantly to be found in the top ten from *Songs of Praise*. Even those who wouldn't touch renewal with a bargepole are appreciative of the best of its music. There is, of course, a certain amount of rubbish, but then there is quite a bit in the old hymn books, too, so that argument cuts both ways.

Charismatics take their time over praise, since it is such an important thing to do: the only important thing, actually, since it's the only thing we'll be doing in heaven. While they are very keen on mission and evangelism, as we'll see in a moment, and are indeed often the most effective at it, charismatics are not generally convinced that mission is the single greatest task of the church, that the church exists by mission as fire exists by burning, that the Great Commission is the most important paragraph in the Bible, and so on. Worship is the highest priority, and because it is so important charismatics want to do all they can to draw every creature, nation, tribe and language into their worship: only then will God have what he desires and deserves, the adoration of all creation. Mission is only the means to the end: worship is our central and eternal duty and joy.

So worship is given the time and effort it deserves. In many churches worship equals singing, and every service may begin with half an hour or more of 'worship slot': one song following another and leading people smoothly, logically and gradually into the intimate presence of God. In other churches, those which are blessed (or stuck, depending on your point of view) with liturgy, the worship is done with more of a structured framework, and uses speech and even action as well as song. But however it is done, this praise is genuine, emotional, heartfelt and real. To remove praise from charismatic spirituality would be to rob it of perhaps its major identity.

These, then, are McDonnell's three characteristics of renewal spirituality: presence, power and praise. But I want to add a fourth and a fifth 'P' to end this section because I believe there are a couple more unsung but vitally important ingredients in renewal spirituality.

Play

What I mean by this is that charismatics don't always take themselves too seriously. They're not, they hope, irreverent, unsound or lax, but they don't always treat their faith with the concern for getting it all exactly right which they might, if pressed, call 'neurotic' in other Christians. They seek to be scrupulously biblical, but they wouldn't usually go to the stake for a particular interpretation or doctrine. They tend to be slightly more comfortable than some with provisionality, keeping options open and hedging bets. Some Christians are terrified of getting into something new in case it might be unsound; charismatics will tend to go for it first and ask questions later. This difference in attitude came to the fore particularly with the advent of the so-called 'Toronto Blessing' in the mid 1990s. Some dived right into the river, while others stood on the shores, needing proof that there were Bible verses to tell them that it was OK to fall over or laugh before they'd so much as get their toes wet.

In other words (and this will sound highly irreverent to some), to the charismatic the Christian faith is a bit of a game. Not in the sense that it doesn't really matter: it clearly does, eternally. Rather, it's that it is possible to get just a bit too po-faced about God and our relationship with him, and didn't it all ought to be just a little bit more fun than others have often made it out to be?

All this is tied in, I think, with the loss of the Christian Sabbath or day of rest. Robert Warren puts it down to the way in which our Bible had its chapter and verse divisions made, back in the sixteenth century, not always as helpfully as might have been. In particular he draws our attention to the division between Genesis 1 and 2. We clearly have two different accounts of the creation, written at different periods in the history of Israel, but the second account begins not in 2:1, as we might logically expect, but for some unknown reason in 2:4. What this means is that the chapter 1 account, with its logical process through the days and the repeated refrain 'And there was evening, and there was morning – the nth day' ends on day six, not day seven. The climax to the chapter is humankind working, giving us the impression that this was the climax of the whole of creation. God resting and celebrating on day seven is a kind of unimportant PS tagged on at the beginning of chapter 2. Robert Warren suggests that 'Placing the chapter break where it belongs, after day seven, reveals the climax of creation not as man-in-dominion but as God-in-celebration. What is now needed is a protestant play-ethic.'[7]

In other words, we have lost the ability in the church to celebrate, play, have fun and generally mess around, and in losing this
we have thought we are being especially close and pleasing to God.
Charismatic renewal says that the truth is very different, and that
our Father God likes nothing more than to watch his children
enjoying themselves. 'If you parents, though you are evil,' Jesus
might have said, 'know how to let your children have fun, how
much more will your heavenly Father let you have fun!'

This principle is seen in action in Luke's famous story of the two
sons in chapter 15. What was it, exactly, that the younger son had
done wrong? The obvious answer is that he had partied! Yet if that
was so sinful, why was it that his father's immediate response to his
homecoming was to throw a party? His instinct for celebration was
obviously not misguided; rather, it was his choice of venue which
was wrong. He felt that in order to celebrate he had to go into a far
country, away from his father. This is surely a picture of the rather
schizophrenic attitude which is so prevalent in the church that
'God' and 'having fun' are mutually exclusive. To learn to celebrate
in the presence of the Father is surely a skill which we in the church
today need urgently to rediscover, and it is a skill which is at least
being worked on in charismatic renewal. Many critics asked of the
Toronto Blessing phase: 'What does it mean? All this laughter, all
this wild behaviour in worship: where is that in the Bible?' One
answer is that it doesn't have to mean anything: it's just such good
fun! To enjoy partying in God's presence may not be a heretical
diversion from the serious business of being Christian: rather, it
may represent something of a homecoming.

Another picture I often use of renewal is that it is the 'jazz' of
spirituality. Musicians in orchestras have to do it by the book: they
must play exactly what the score tells them to, no more, no less.
But jazz musicians have an entirely different philosophy of music.
There is a framework, a structure, but within that structure they are
free to make it up as they go along. Improvisation is the name of
the game, and the real beauty of the music lies in the spontaneity
which puts flesh on the bare bones of the harmonic structure. Some
solos are, no doubt, more effective than others, and some might not
even work at all. But that doesn't matter; it is the art-form as a

whole which has its value, a value much greater than the individual contributions to it.

The other thing to note about jazz is that it isn't always as easy to tell what has worked and what hasn't. When you're playing from a score any given note is either right or wrong, and it is a simple matter to decide which. But improvisation is nowhere near as clear-cut. Indeed, much music gets its beauty from suspension and resolution, the use of notes which don't fit but which move to become ones which do. Some Christians have a mindset which demands that everything must be 'right': doctrinally sound, thoroughly biblical, liturgically correct and totally appropriate. Charismatics generally feel much happier with experimentation, risk-taking and provisionality, and have enough faith in God to believe that at the end of the day everything is likely to work out OK, or that if it doesn't God is big enough to correct things and get us back on the right track. This sounds notoriously dangerous to some, and of course there are instances of charismatics going wildly wrong and moving into heresy, but that doesn't usually stop them from experimenting. The possibility of error must of course be guarded against, but even temporary error is seen to be preferable to the kind of paralysis which means that we never do very much at all, *in case* it's wrong.

This mindset, of willingness to experiment, has many implications for other areas of Christian discipleship, and it will come up again before this book is finished, but I note it here because I believe it is one of the fundamental characteristics of charismatic spirituality.

Purpose

My fifth 'P' concerns what it is all about. Is charismatic spirituality simply a pietistic, self-indulgent feast on spiritual experience, or an occultish quest for personal spiritual power? While for a minority that might be how it appears, it is my conviction that for main-stream charismatics the very opposite is true. They are out to change the world!

In Acts 1:8 Jesus makes a further promise to his disciples about the coming of the Holy Spirit to them, now only a few days hence.

When that happens, he tells them, they will become his witnesses, moving in ever-increasing circles which will eventually encompass the whole world. The extra ending to St Mark's gospel tells of this same mission, which will be accompanied by the kinds of signs and wonders with which charismatics have been associated. I know that there is some dispute as to whether these few verses tagged on to the end of Mark's gospel are original or whether they were added later, but even if that is true it only goes to prove my point further: someone somewhere in the early church thought that these things ought to have been mentioned, presumably because they were common practice in the church, and so took the liberty of adding them.

So there is a clear link between the Spirit and the mission of the church, a link which remains, I believe, to this day. I believe that it is true to say that where churches welcome the charismatic activity of the Holy Spirit they will be more likely to be vibrant, growing and healthy, provided other leadership factors are in place; and where the church deliberately shuts out the Spirit, or places severe limitations on what he is allowed to do, that church is more likely to head for decline and death.

I said something very like this a few years ago in the *Church Times*, an august and venerable Anglican newspaper, and as you might imagine I was thoroughly taken to the cleaners for daring to make such an outrageous statement! Several letters put me right, either through the columns of the paper the next week or privately to my office, about the fact that there were plenty of charismatic churches in sad decline, and many non-charismatic churches doing very nicely indeed, thank you very much. All that is of course true, but not one of the many people who wrote to me seemed to have noticed one word which I wrote clearly into my article, the word 'world-wide'. The problem with living in England is that I can so easily think that the rest of the world is pretty much the same as my home country: in fact, nothing could be further from the truth.

In some other parts of the world, and particularly in the developing countries, the church is healthy, vibrant, growing numerically and radically affecting the communities in which it is set. There is fervent day-and-night prayer and intercession; there are radical reconciliation and justice initiatives; there is political involvement;

and Christians are respected as those with real spiritual authority, even if those who respect them would also like to wipe them from the face of the earth. And the church in such places is almost certain to be charismatic or Pentecostal, and to have an expectation that the power of the Spirit to heal, to deliver and to change lives will be normative.

In some areas whole cities are being taken for the kingdom of God, and the Christians find favour in the eyes of the secular community and its officials and are invited to contribute a spiritual agenda to the secular life of the city. Literally thousands are being won to Christ daily, and as a result the crime rate is dropping, health care, education and other social conditions are improving, prisons are emptying, illicit drugs are disappearing from the streets, and the *shalom*, or peace and harmony, of God is descending on the community. And wherever this is happening, charismatics are at the forefront of it. For Christians living in England it is easy to assume that what we see here is an accurate picture of the church world-wide: the fact is that the British church is the armpit of the Body of Christ. Make no mistake: on a world-wide scale, charismatic renewal works!

And, it has to be said, it isn't doing *that* badly here at home. Where there is a significantly large church, it is very likely to be a charismatic church: the exceptions would be large evangelical churches built on their preaching ministry, which do seem to be able to grow if there is a university within easy reach. The phenomenal rise of the House or New Churches, which are almost all distinctly charismatic, shows the appeal of renewal, even if some would regard them as less helpful in other ways. From the renewal stable have come the phenomenally successful 'Alpha' course, through which thousands have been won to a Christian faith, 'Emmaus', the slightly more broadly based Anglican course based on some Roman Catholic ideas, Anglican Renewal Ministries' own 'Saints Alive!', and several other evangelistic packages which God has been pleased to use for his kingdom. Youth congregations, which are bucking the trends and holding on to teenagers where they traditionally would have disappeared at about the age of 12, are likely to have come from a charismatic background, and the teenagers they keep are signifi-cantly more likely to be involved up to the hilt in intercession, evangelism and other areas of ministry. The charismatic-based work of Fusion is revolutionizing evangelistic work among students, with tremendous success.

Closely, although not exclusively, allied with the charismatic scene have been initiatives such as March for Jesus, Church Planting, Cell Church and any number of projects involved in prayer and intercession, all of which represent a gathering head of steam towards the revival of Britain. Of course there are good things happening outside renewal; of course not all charismatic churches or organizations are necessarily healthy and vibrant, but many which are healthy and vibrant are statistically likely to be charismatic to some degree. I'll return to this subject in rather more detail later.

Charismatics, then, really do seem to be driven by an agenda more wide than their own personal desire for a bless-up. They see a town, or a city, or even a nation out there to be won for the kingdom, and they are more than likely to be among the forefront of those going for it. This 'purpose' characteristic of renewal is vitally important – and when you think about it, isn't that exactly what you would be led to expect if you looked at much of what the New Testament says about the Holy Spirit?

So charismatics can be defined as having these five elements to their spirituality: presence, power, praise, play and purpose. I hope that by now you have some sense of what we're discussing in this book, even if you don't much like the sound of it. We'll move on now into the next section, where I will try to convince you that 'being charismatic' is not something which we are free to pick and choose as we like, but that it is a central and non-negotiable part of normal Christian discipleship.

Before we move on, though, this might be a good point to clarify some terminology. I have already drawn a distinction between the Pentecostal denominations and the charismatic movement, but from now on that distinction may get a bit blurred from time to time. Clearly there are some doctrinal differences between Pentecostalism and charismatic renewal, and also a huge ecclesiological difference (that just means the ways they understand church and church organization). But in terms of spirituality there is far more in common between the two groupings than there is to divide them.

Most theologians speak of 'charismatics' and 'pentecostals' inter-changeably; many indeed join the two words together and talk about pentecostal/charismatic spirituality. From now on I shall do the same, adding a third term, 'renewal', to mean pretty much the same thing. So when I talk specifically about the Pentecostal denominations, I shall use a capital 'P'. A lower-case 'p' means that I am referring to the spirituality and not to a specific church grouping. I hope that makes sense: on with the task!

Part Two

. . . .

Why Me?

Chapter 5

In at the Deep End

So here we go. It will help us through this section if we see the different chapters as contributing different answers to the question 'Why should I be charismatic?' Let's begin at the beginning with the first answer to that question: 'Because that's what your baptism was all about'.

We humans love initiation ceremonies. Beavers get pulled on a rope up to Cubs; Brownies jump over toadstools to become Guides; new pupils at schools get some kind of ill-treatment (mine was to have newly cut grass stuffed inside my trousers and shirt: others apparently endure much worse). If you wanted to join one ancient Roman religion you went through the *taurobolium*: you were put into a pit over which a bull was suspended, and the bull then had its throat cut so that the blood poured out all over you. Masons roll up their trouser-legs, so I'm informed; monarchs are crowned; priests are ordained; so the list goes on. In each case the move into a new role, status or position is signified by some kind of a ritual, where the candidate's change in lifestyle is publicly marked.

It was John the Baptist who first practised baptism as the initiation ceremony into the Christian life. In fact, some kind of washing was not an uncommon ceremony in different religions, and a form of baptism was used for Gentiles who wanted to associate themselves with the Jewish community without going the whole hog and undergoing the official initiation ceremony of circumcision (for which who can blame them?). Since the days of John, baptism has been seen as *the* initiation ceremony for followers of Jesus, who himself submitted to it, even though the cleansing of which it spoke was irrelevant to him as the sinless Son of God.

So what is baptism, and what is its link with the Holy Spirit?

The symbolism of baptism

Despite differences of opinion in the church about the age at which it should be administered and the quantity of water to be used, all agree that the use of water on a candidate speaks of two different areas of symbolism, washing and drowning. Some see it primarily as John would no doubt have seen it, as a cleansing from a sinful lifestyle and a preparation for something different in the future. If a day spent gardening or under the car is to be followed by an intimate evening out with my wife, a turning point is required: a nice hot shower and a change of clothes marks the transition from garden or garage to restaurant. In the same way John called those who heeded his message of the need for repentance to be washed clean from the lifestyle they had lived, and the way they had been dirtied and tainted by their sins. After their baptism, they were to live in a different way, proving by their deeds that their change of heart had been genuine.

But Jesus' life and death gave baptism a whole new meaning, a meaning which some of the later New Testament writers were quick to pick up on. Our sins were not as easy as that to deal with: we needed more than a wash. If I spill coffee down one of my white shirts, it is fairly easy to remedy: my wife washes it, and it's as good as new. But some strains of lamb vindaloo which from time to time have found their way on to my clothing present much more of a problem: often the best I can do is to buy a new shirt and use the old one for cleaning the car (first cutting out the stained bit, of course, lest it should attack the paintwork). According to some bits of the Bible, our sin is of such a severe nature that mere washing is not enough: we need to be drowned, and to rise again as brand new people. The water of baptism is seen as a parallel to the burial of Jesus: just as he died, was buried and rose again, so we die to the old life of sin and selfishness, are 'buried at sea' in the waters of baptism, and rise again as completely different people. 'If anyone is in Christ,' wrote St Paul to his Corinthian friends, 'he is a new creation; the old has gone, the new has come!' (2 Corinthians 5:17)

But there is a third area of symbolism attached to baptism by the New Testament writers. The word itself, as we have seen, means to drench, plunge, or immerse something in something else, and John explained to those whom he drenched with water that this ceremony was only a picture of another drenching which was to follow. He was able only to complete the outward ceremony, but someone was coming close behind him who would drench people not with water but with Holy Spirit, an inner baptism which would cover people not with water but with the power of God.

This dual baptism for those who were willing to turn from their sins led to what Bible-teacher David Pawson argues coherently was the 'normal Christian birth', or the usual process of initiation for new Christians.[1] This was a four-part cluster of repenting, believing, being baptized in water, and being baptized in Holy Spirit.

But if this was the normal pattern for initiation, there were exceptions, examples where for one reason or another things didn't quite follow the normal pattern. One such exception is recorded for us in Acts 19, and it is fascinating to look more closely at this passage. Paul visits Ephesus, and finds some 'disciples' (people who had already started following the way of Jesus). But something about them obviously struck him as slightly wrong, so he asked them if they had received the Holy Spirit when they had first believed. 'We've not even heard that there is a Holy Spirit!' came the reply. Here were some people who had believed in Jesus (presumably repenting of their sins to do so) and were actively engaged in following him, but who had never heard of the Holy Spirit (actually the Greek text may mean something a bit more like 'We've never even heard that the Holy Spirit is available to us' but the gist of the passage is the same).

Now at this point Paul asks an interesting question. We might expect him to have asked something like 'Who on earth was your minister/vicar/pastor/leader, if he never even told you about the Holy Spirit?' or 'Who took your confirmation classes?!' or even 'Which evangelist did you respond to?' But the question is different: 'What baptism did you receive?' This is highly significant: it seems to imply that the Holy Spirit ought to have been available to them in some way through the ceremony of baptism. If I returned home with a new car and my wife asked me if I had filled it with petrol yet, and I told her that I'd never ever heard there was such a thing as petrol, she might justifiably ask me whatever garage did I get the car from. Wasn't I told that a car required petrol to make it go? Didn't they even send me away with a tankful? In the same way Paul's question seems to suggest that a baptism which doesn't even introduce people to the Spirit, let alone enable them to receive him, is a very substandard baptism indeed.

The British church today is packed full of Christians like those Ephesians. There are countless numbers of Christians who have been baptized in water but have never been introduced to the person and work of the Holy Spirit other than as an interesting piece of theology or a slightly scary 'ghost'. They are trying as sincerely as they can to follow Jesus, but without any functional understanding or experience of the Holy Spirit. According to Paul's reaction, baptism ought to have delivered the goods, but was done in such a way that it simply hadn't.

But how was a physical baptism in water meant to produce a spiritual baptism in Holy Spirit? This is less clear from the Bible. In the case of Jesus' baptism it was a spontaneous event which happened as he was coming up out of the water of the River Jordan. In other examples, such as that in the chapter of Acts we're looking at, the water-baptism was followed by prayer and the laying-on of hands for the baptism in the Spirit. David Pawson, after examining all the evidence, concludes that this was the most usual pattern: after someone repented of their sins and put their faith in Jesus they would receive water-baptism followed immediately by prayer for the gift of the Spirit. It was exactly this pattern, he argues, which much later was to become institutionalized into the Anglican practice of Confirmation, when after baptism (usually a very long time after) the bishop would lay hands on people and pray for the gift of the Holy Spirit to be given to them.

If all this is true, it has some very serious implications for the baptism which is practised in most churches today. If it was the case that the ceremony of baptism ought to include a part which actually 'gave' the Holy Spirit to people, we have some serious questions to answer about why that apparently does not happen very often nowadays.

Baptism and the gift of the Spirit

The most obvious answer to that question, and the answer which makes sense of the words of the Bible and of the liturgy used in some churches for baptisms, is that actually it *does* procure the gift of the Spirit. Then why does nothing appear to happen? The first possibility, of course, is that those we baptize have not really repented or believed, so that their baptism is only an empty ceremony which can't possibly deliver the goods of the Spirit. This argument is often used by those whose church tradition would not allow the baptism of babies: since they cannot have repented or believed, they can't possibly receive the Spirit. It's not the purpose of this book to argue for or against infant baptism, so I'll sidestep that question and ask another: what of those who *are* appropriate candidates for baptism, who have repented and believed but who still, as a result of their baptism, show no outward signs of having received the Spirit? There are still plenty of people in that category! Why do we see no evidence of the Spirit at work in cases like that, or at least not the same kind of evidence that we see in the book of Acts? (More of this in a moment.)

This is an important question, and different groups have answered it in different ways. We've already mentioned the belief in the early Pentecostal churches that there is a kind of two-stage initiation: first of all we receive the Spirit for conversion, and he enters our lives bringing new birth in Christ, but that has to be followed subsequently, and perhaps some time subsequently, by a 'Second Blessing', at which the Spirit enters us with empowerment for ministry and service. This view is based on the passages from Acts we have looked at, where that is exactly what has happened. Some strands of Pentecostalism would even go on to talk about a 'Third Blessing' for sanctification, as the Spirit begins work on our character and Christian lifestyle.

Nowadays, however, most Christians (including many Pentecostals) would reject this view. While in the Bible it *does* appear to happen that way on a couple of occasions, that isn't to say that it is what the Bible teaches *should* happen. In other words, the Acts passages about subsequent reception of the Spirit some time after conversion are not paradigms or models which we're meant to follow; they are rather exceptions, describing what happened when something had gone wrong.

Other biblical material is, frankly, a bit confusing on this issue. The three main New Testament writers to deal with the Holy Spirit in any detail are Paul, John and Luke. Theologian Max Turner notes that for Paul the gift of the Spirit is primarily to do with salvation. Quoting Gordon Fee, a Pentecostal scholar, he asserts that

> The gift of the Spirit for Paul is manifestly the power of the believers' salvation, 'the absolutely essential constituent of the whole Christian life'. Christian life begins by the Spirit (2 Cor. 3; Gal. 3:3–5), is sustained by the Spirit in the fight against the 'flesh' (Gal. 3:5–6; Rom. 8), and in the renewed 'fellowship' of the community (Phil. 2:1; 2 Cor. 13:13) as one body ... and it will be consummated by the Spirit (1 Cor. 15) who is the 'first instalment' of the believers' resurrection life.[2]

When we look at the writings of John the picture is more confusing, as he seems to be saying clearly that the Spirit does come in two stages, as it were. First the Spirit is given to Jesus' disciples, at different points throughout his ministry but most decisively in John 20:22. But Jesus also promises that once he has ascended to heaven the Spirit will come to replace him as the one who will bring his followers into contact with the Father and who will drive their mission and witness in the world. However, Turner argues that what was true for the first disciples cannot be the expected pattern for believers after them. Future Christians would receive the Spirit once, for both salvation and empowerment.[3]

Moving on to Luke, the writer of the book of Acts, Turner finds no conflict between his emphasis on the Spirit as the one who empowers believers for mission and witness and the more salvation-based spin given by Paul and, to some degree, John. Rejecting a two-stage model, he explains that all those who are alive in Christ as genuine Christians have received the Spirit, whether or not they look and behave like charismatics:

> It is conventional in many circles to classify Charismatic and 'non-charismatic' churches on the basis of whether they experience tongues, prophecy and healing. But this is far too narrow a basis, obscuring the much wider range of gifts that flow from the Spirit ... [In many other churches] the charismatic Spirit of prophecy enlivens and directs the church through other gifts, granting illumination of Scripture in preaching, wisdom and understanding in Bible study; a deep sense of God's presence and guidance in corporate and individual prayer, and so forth ... There are perhaps churches that are all but dead, and in which, alas, one never senses anything that transcends ordinary human possibilities with an awareness of God. But wherever God is sensed, he is made known only in and through the Spirit of prophecy.[4]

Turner would tell us, therefore, that it isn't true to say that a charismatic is someone who has received the Spirit while a non-charismatic hasn't, nor is it true to say that a charismatic has somehow received *more* of the Spirit than a non-charismatic. So what is the difference, because there clearly is one! Just what exactly am I writing this book urging people to do?

Unwrapping the gifts

I find the most helpful concept one of 'release'. You won't find this directly in the Bible, but it does seem to describe the experience in a way which takes seriously the careful examination of the Bible by theologians like Turner and Fee. The Spirit is given to us, if we're Christians, once and once only, and when we receive him we get all we need for being born into life with Christ. We become Christians, are born again, or whatever you want to call it, and as the Spirit takes up residence in our lives he brings with him all his gifts, and makes them available to us. It's your birthday, there's a knock at the door, and standing there is a friend with his arms laden with presents for you. You invite him in, but you do then need to set about the task of unwrapping the presents and putting them to use. A non-charismatic isn't someone who has never received the friend or his gifts: rather he or she is someone who hasn't yet unwrapped some of the presents. This may be for a variety of reasons: for some, certain of the gifts may be down behind the settee somewhere and simply haven't been noticed yet. When their presence is pointed out, they are grabbed eagerly. But for others it may be a policy decision not to unwrap some presents, based on a variety of beliefs such as a conviction that they don't really exist nowadays, or that they'll harm me if I open them, or even that I've met someone else with that gift and the last thing I'd want is to be like them! So the presents remain unopened, and the recipients would proudly call themselves Christians but equally proudly claim not to be charismatic. 'My gift is flower-arranging,' the rhetoric goes, 'so don't come near me with any of that supernatural stuff!'

If all this is true I am arguing in this book not for a 'new' or 'second' experience of the Holy Spirit, but simply that we gladly embrace all that he might want to do through us – all, in fact, that our baptism is meant to provide us with – rather than ignoring or neglecting some of his gifts, usually the more dramatic and spectacular ones. Our history lesson in Chapter 3 showed us that the church has successfully 'tamed' the Holy Spirit at times, but that in the twentieth century some lost gifts were rediscovered. So the exuberance and joy of charismatics who have rediscovered more from God is not primarily that of a new experience of the Spirit; rather, it is the excitement of children who have suddenly discovered a whole load more presents hidden away just when they thought they'd finished and opened all there was for them.

Going public

There is one more side-effect of this taming of the Spirit, though, which we need to look at before summing up this chapter, and it concerns the contrast between the joyful and often dramatic nature of baptism and the reception of the Spirit in the Bible, and the rather sedate experience of most Christians today. If a cluster of repenting, believing, water-baptism and prayer for baptism in the Holy Spirit is the New Testament norm, why is so much baptism in today's church such an apparent non-event? Quite simply, the argument goes, because the Spirit is given inwardly and secretly: the water-baptism is the outward ceremony which other people may see and which the candidate may feel, but the giving of the Spirit is an inner, hidden transaction which is not on public view. If you were to ask most people whether or not they received the Spirit at their baptism you would get one of two answers: either 'I'm not sure,' or 'Yes, of course I must have done, because that's what baptism does!'

This sounds reasonable, except for one thing: David Pawson argues, convincingly to my mind, that on every single occasion in the New Testament in which we are told of people receiving the Spirit, it was a publicly visible, or at least a publicly audible, event. In Acts 19 the newly baptized disciples spoke in tongues and prophesied, and one or both of these verbal outpourings were present either directly or by implication in every such event recorded for us. When Jesus was baptized there was an audible voice from heaven, but on every other occasion something public and audible happened to and from the candidates. The disciples on the day of Pentecost spoke in tongues. Paul, as a result of his prayer for the Spirit in Acts 9, spoke in tongues more than any of the Corinthians (a church renowned for their excessive and inappropriate use of the gift). The Samaritan Christians in Acts 8, disciples who like the Ephesians had missed out on their full initiation, reacted powerfully and visibly to the coming of the Spirit: we're not told specifically that they spoke in tongues, but they did do something dramatic, such that Simon the Magician wanted to buy the ability to make people behave like that, since no doubt it would have enhanced his magic shows. Pawson concludes that true baptism in the Spirit is an event which it is impossible to miss! The privatized 'inner' reception of the Spirit claimed by many today, a reception which seems to make no apparent difference at all, has absolutely no precedent in the New Testament.

But you've just argued that we *do* receive the Spirit when we become Christians, I hear you cry. Now are you saying that unless it's all noisy we haven't received him after all? No, not quite, but I am saying that I believe that in the church we have institutionalized the neglect of certain of the Spirit's gifts, such that it has become the norm not to do anything noisy! We have told the Spirit what he is and isn't allowed to do: it's fine to gift me with biblical insight or practical skills to be used within the life of the church, but please keep the supernatural stuff away. So baptism, which in the New Testament seems often to have been a joyously supernatural affair, leaving no-one in any doubt that God had *done* something, becomes institutionalized in the church into a quiet little ceremony which rocks no boats, makes no waves and leaves everyone with little evidence that anything at all has happened.

Filling the gaps

What then are we to make of the two Acts passages, Acts 8 and 19? I think we only have three options, and I'm not willing to come down clearly on any one of them. The first is that their filling with the Spirit was an initial conversion. They may have 'received the word' or been 'learning' from Christ (that's what 'disciples' do), but they had never actually reached the point of repentance and faith. The apostles in effect helped them over the line into relationship with Jesus and membership of the kingdom of God. Their filling with the Spirit was the normal experience which every New Testament believer would have experienced.

Second, they may have been genuine Christians who neverthe-less needed to experience the 'release' of supernatural spiritual gifts. Their filling with the Spirit in the passages in question was not an initial reception, but one of the 'toppings up' which we're all called to experience regularly (Ephesians 5:18 – more on this later). In either case I would argue that there are plenty of people in today's church in both these places.

The third possibility, finally, is that for some reason these two groups of people did indeed have a second and subsequent 'blessing', perhaps a bit like that message you get on your computer screen from time to time: 'This programme was not installed correctly. Please run set-up again.' However, to build a theology and practice on this understanding is to base our doctrine on a couple of mistakes! I don't know which is the correct answer, but at the end of the day I'm not that bothered: my desire is to see Christians filled with the fullness of God, and receiving all he's got for them.

All this has, it seems to me, serious implications for the church today. If it is true that there are many people about who think they might have received the Spirit but have no evidence to back that opinion up, what are we to do about that? Yes, it might be the case for some of them that they are not really Christians, not having repented and believed in Jesus, but what of the rest? Many people have been following Jesus faithfully for decades, growing in knowledge and grace and serving him effectively in the life of the church, winning others to him by their witness, even leading churches into growth and health, but would claim no specific time or no concrete evidence that they have ever had a supernatural experience of having been filled with or baptized in the Holy Spirit. What of them?

In the early days of the British charismatic movement, in the sixties and early seventies, there was a tremendous amount of arrogance on the part of those who had recently come into a fresh experience of being filled with the Spirit. Those who hadn't had such an experience felt themselves branded as 'second-class' Christians, not quite up to the mark, and not as dear to God as those who had received a charismatic experience. Fortunately charismatics have learnt some lessons from that time and now realize that the experience of receiving specific and dramatic gifts is not the only mark of Christian discipleship. They have become much more able to celebrate and recognize other areas of the Spirit's work in people: no longer do they tend to regard mature and experienced Christians who happen not to have had this 'baptism in the Spirit' as totally spiritually bankrupt. This is all to the good, but the down side is that we have forgotten to challenge people lovingly, and to suggest that there might be more for them to receive from God. There may be presents as yet unwrapped.

When I'm speaking I often illustrate this point by using Lego bricks. Imagine that full Christian maturity is like building a brick wall. Along the base of the wall are the foundation stones, each representing a different aspect of Christian discipleship. Such stones might be labelled 'prayer', 'worship', 'service', 'Holy Spirit', 'witness', 'giving', 'Bible knowledge', 'holiness' and so on.

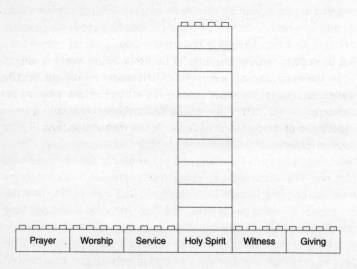

| Prayer | Worship | Service | Holy Spirit | Witness | Giving |

What happened to some new Christians in the seventies was that they suddenly experienced the baptism in the Spirit, and quickly began to grow proficient in the use of the 1 Corinthians 12 gifts of the Spirit. Their brick wall might have looked like this: a huge tower built on that particular foundation stone, but with very little growth and maturity elsewhere.

| Prayer | Worship | Service | Holy Spirit | Witness | Giving |

Not much of a wall, really, is it? It's certainly not a structure from which they could look arrogantly down on others.

But others, who had been faithfully following Jesus for years and who had achieved a high degree of maturity in other areas had, to all intents and purposes, 'not even heard that there was a Holy Spirit'. Their wall looked like this: pretty high but still with a huge gap in the middle.

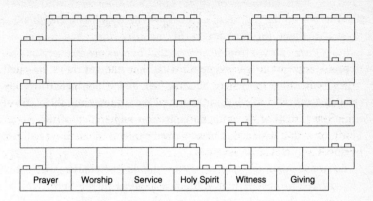

| Prayer | Worship | Service | Holy Spirit | Witness | Giving |

At the end of the day, there really isn't much to choose between the two walls: neither of them is complete, and the builders of either one have little to be proud of over the other. Full maturity, a complete brick wall, looks like this, with the 'Spirit' column taking its place alongside other areas of growth and maturity to form a sturdy and effective wall.

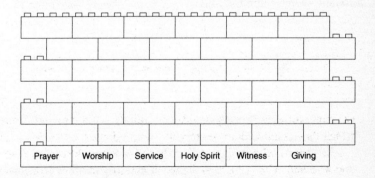

| Prayer | Worship | Service | Holy Spirit | Witness | Giving |

So charismatics nowadays may have learnt not to look down with arrogance on those who have their 'Spirit' column unbuilt, but they have equally forgotten, for fear of retreating into an arrogant position, to remind others that there is a missing dimension in their discipleship.

When Paul encountered those Ephesian Christians who were missing out on the resources of the Spirit, he wasn't content simply to praise them for the degree of maturity they had achieved (although we can see from his letters that he was always very quick to praise and encourage people for what they had got right): he saw a situation which needed to be remedied, and which needed to be remedied quickly! For him, it simply wasn't good enough to continue the Christian life with no conscious experience of the Holy Spirit, or with a whole load of neglected presents: something had to be done!

So to ask again our question 'Why should I be charismatic?', we would have to answer that without a baptism in the Spirit which delivers all the goods, and not just the ones which are socially acceptable to a largely dying church, our Christian initiation, and in particular our water-baptism, is incomplete and inadequate. The Bible seems to make it clear that reception of the Spirit and experience of his gifts, in a way which it is impossible to miss, is something which baptism ought to include. If your baptism didn't include it, if you can't say with certainty that you have consciously and specifically been filled with the Spirit in a way which left you different, there's more for you!

Chapter 6

Blessed Assurance

In sixteen years of parish ministry, one of the most common issues I faced among the people I was serving was that of insecurity. I'm not just talking about insecurity on a human level, although there was plenty of that too, but primarily about insecurity with God. To put it crudely, people were not sure whether they were going to heaven or not. Ask the average Christian if they are sure of a place in heaven, and most often you'll get answers like 'I hope so' or 'I'm trying to be good enough' or 'I do/don't feel I deserve to.' Some people even feel that it is arrogant and presumptuous to be certain that they are accepted by God, and that to claim this for themselves is tantamount to saying that they are somehow perfect, or at least better than the average.

I believe that this uncertainty is at the root of a huge malaise in the churches of our land. What it means, simply, is that many church members are so busy *trying* to be Christians that they never actually *are* Christians. In the past I applied for a job which I very much wanted. I was selected for interview, and because the job meant so much to me I tried as hard as I could to impress the panel – put on a suit and tie, went out of my way to look intelligent, to give the answers I thought they wanted to hear, and so on. The net result was that I was a nervous wreck, stuttered my way through the interview, got thoroughly confused and came in third out of three. More recently I was again being interviewed for a job, but this time it was very different. A series of dramatic and clearly divine experiences, and several prophetic words given to me, had shown me clearly that this was the job for me. The crowning glory to all this divine revelation came a few days before the interview, when a wise lady in our congregation, whom I would have trusted with my life, told me that God had told her to tell me that I was going to be appointed and that it was his will for me. Now, of course, to rely too heavily on that kind of guidance can be a recipe for disaster and deep disappointment, but the clarity of the words I had received, the trusted people through whom I had received them, and the sheer weight of evidence felt to me totally convincing. As you might imagine, I went into the interview with a certain confidence which I had not had on the previous occasion, and I got the job!

Amazing grace

Many Christians would desperately like to be right with God, but have no evidence at all that they actually are. So they nervously make their way through their Christian lives, desperately trying to impress God and desperately scared in case they don't. We even make a virtue out of our uncertainty, which breeds a spirituality based on excessive self-abasement. The returning prodigal son in Luke chapter 15, when rehearsing his little speech, says 'Father' but actually means 'Boss', since he feels no security in his relationship and expects to be treated from that point on merely as an employee. 'I am not worthy' becomes the watchword, or, as Anglicans might say, 'We do not presume'. Life becomes a grovel before the Almighty, and heaven becomes a desperate hope rather than an exciting certainty. We don't *belong* to God; we merely work for him.

There are two reasons for this scary and defective spirituality: one doctrinal and one experiential. The doctrinal one is about grace, and it is not a new problem. Our insecurity comes because our working model is that we can get ourselves into God's good books and thence into heaven, and Christians since the earliest times have struggled with this issue. The Christian gospel is that we are not worthy, but that because of what Jesus has done we are accepted anyway. Our salvation is by grace, through faith; in other words Jesus saves us even though we don't deserve it, and he saves us when we put our trust in him and in his way of saving us. Our sinfulness separates us from a holy God, but Jesus took our sins, nailed them to the cross, and instead has given us his righteousness, his perfection. We don't deserve this to have happened, any more than that son deserved his father's forgiveness after slapping him in the face and blowing his fortune. It is only by grace.

For years I'd known about grace in theory, and had heard preachers say things like

God's
Riches
At
Christ's
Expense

which, if I'm honest, confused me even more. It was only a few years ago that I really understood it as I heard my little daughter singing a song she had learnt from a tape, the words of which went something like this:

Grace is when God gives us
The things we don't deserve
He does it because he loves us.

A helpful second verse adds

Mercy is when God does not
Give us what we deserve!
He does it because he loves us.[1]

Suddenly it all became clear: when God chooses to withhold the punishment which should rightly be mine, and instead gives me blessings which there is no way I should be getting, I am subject both to his mercy and to his grace. I long that other Christians should grasp this simple truth. Our security is not based on what we can do, but rather on what Jesus has done and what we have believed about it. If our salvation depended on our own capacity for making the grade, it would indeed be arrogant to suggest that

57

without doubt we were destined for heaven. If I emerge from an exam feeling I've got an A* and then go round telling everyone, I might well be setting myself up for a fall and looking very stupid in the process. But Christianity isn't an exam: because we can claim no credit ourselves assurance is not arrogant. We can rejoice in something given to us as a free gift far more appropriately than we can in something we have gained ourselves.

This is the argument of large chunks of the New Testament, and in particular the letter to the Galatians. They had begun in grace and faith, but had taken the retrograde step into trying to please God by keeping the Jewish law and working at their own salvation. Paul has some extremely strong things to say about their foolishness in taking this step, and encourages them to remember that it is Jesus who has won their salvation and who gave it to them as a free gift.

I wonder what Paul would have to say if he were to write a letter to the church today. This problem is endemic, and I suspect he would need to be even more strong in countering it. And yet it seems to be so deeply ingrained in us that we often don't even hear, let alone grasp, what good news the gospel of grace really is. I can remember as a young and enthusiastic curate preaching a real rip-roaring sermon on this theme, telling people that they could never ever please God by their own efforts but that their salvation was assured if only they would stop trying, admit their bankruptcy and put their trust in Jesus and in what he did for them on the cross. On and on I went, spelling it all out as clearly as I knew how, and labouring the point until I was sure even an intelligent chimp who may have wandered in by mistake would have got it. But in the porch after the service a elderly gentleman who was visiting the church stopped to congratulate me on my fine sermon. 'That was absolutely wonderful,' he said. 'It really helped me to understand things in a way I've never grasped before, and so from now on I'm going to work as hard as I can so that one day I might just get to heaven!' The grace of God was further in evidence as I managed to refrain from giving him a severe slapping, but it was a close thing!

What a glorious liberation it is when we really grasp the doctrine of grace! All our insecurity vanishes as the truth dawns upon us: it's not up to me! Jesus has done it for me! If only we could grasp and teach this truth in the church, we'd be so different. All the 'I'm not worthy' grovelling before God would vanish, and all the effort and anxiety expended on trying to be a Christian could be spent on being one. The interview is over, the job is in the bag, so let's get on with doing it!

More than doctrine

To preach and teach right doctrine over this matter would be tremendously liberating for the church, but there is an even deeper need and an even more important priority. The fact is, whether we like it or not, that we sometimes need more than doctrine: propositional truth is not always enough. Fortunately God has provided something else for us to refresh the parts biblical truth can't reach: personal experience.

In explaining what I mean by this, I want to note first of all that the biblical writers felt it important that we *know* where we stand with God. John wrote his short first letter all about *knowing*: related words appear thirty-two times, and again and again like a refrain comes the phrase 'This is how we *know*...' He seems to have been writing to uncertain Christians, and he is very concerned indeed that they know. 'I write these things to you who believe in the name of the Son of God so that you may know that you have eternal life' says John in his key verse (1 John 5:13). In the logic of his argument, he uses three things to help them know: historical facts about Jesus, the evidence of changed lives, and the gift of the Spirit.

First of all he points them to fact, or Christian belief or doctrine. Some things we know because of what Jesus did: we know about love because Jesus showed it by dying for us (1 John 3:16). We know that the Son of God has come (in the flesh) and that fact becomes foundational for our faith (5:20; 4:2). Historical fact provides the foundation for our faith: right doctrine matters. But it isn't the whole story.

Second, he points to the evidence of changed lives. 'We know we have come to know him if we obey his commands,' says John in 2:3. This is echoed in 2:9 where love for fellow-Christians provides the evidence required, and the whole paragraph of 2:12–14 spells out the experience of different age groups. It's not always easy to see this in ourselves, of course, particularly if we are a bit inclined to an I-am-not-worthy mindset. We don't notice our children growing up, because we're with them all the time. It takes a visit to an auntie or someone to help us to see that 'Ooh, haven't they got big!' That's why encouragement in the church is so important: we're too quick to point out one another's faults, but far too slow to tell each other how our lives have changed for the better. To do so can be encouraging not only for its own sake, but also because assurance of where we are with God can come down that route.

But the third and most crucial evidence for our acceptance by God comes through personal experience, and this is where the work of the Spirit comes particularly into play. 'We know that we live in him and he in us,' says John in 4:13, 'because he has given us of his Spirit.' Here, and elsewhere in the New Testament, this argument is used as the ultimate clincher. But can you notice something about it? It only works if you *know* that he *has* given you his Spirit. Imagine the conversation between John and an average member of today's church:

> 'John, I'm having a bit of trouble over this Christianity business. Can I be sure I really am a Christian? Can I know God loves me, and will one day welcome me into heaven?'
>
> 'Yes,' says John, 'you can indeed be sure that you live in God and that he lives in you, because he has given you his Holy Spirit.'
>
> Pause.
>
> 'John, I'm having a bit of trouble over this Holy Spirit business. Can I be sure I really have received the Spirit?'

Paul has a similar conversation in Romans 8. This triumphant climax to seven chapters of explanation of the gospel begins with the thundering assertion 'Therefore, there is now no condemnation for those who are in Christ Jesus.' But it begs the question 'Does that really apply to me? Am I definitely in Christ Jesus?'

'Yes,' says Paul, 'because the Spirit has set you free.'

'But how do I know I've been set free?' the neurotic Christian replies.

'Because your mind is now set on what the Spirit wants, and no longer on what you want.'

'But how do I know that's true?'

'Because it's the Spirit who controls you now.'

'But how do I know the Spirit is controlling me?'

'Easy!' says Paul. 'You're controlled by the Spirit if the Spirit of God lives in you!'

You can just hear the next question, can't you? 'How do I know whether or not the Spirit of God lives in me?'

Isn't it fascinating that neither John nor Paul even considers that as a possible supplementary question? It's clear from reading the texts that the fact of the Spirit's indwelling is without doubt the clincher, after which the only possible response is a sigh of relief and 'That's all right, then!'

You see, this only works if you know you have received, and have some evidence, as it were, to carry around with you. As one who was brought up in the Baptist denomination, I followed their practices and was baptized by total immersion at the age of 17, rather than as an Anglican baby. I have never once doubted that experience, not just because I have a certificate to prove that it happened, but because I was there! It was an unmissable event, and the memory of it convinces me beyond the shadow of a doubt that I am a baptized person. In the same way, I believe, the receiving of the Holy Spirit ought to be an event, and it ought to be the kind of event which leaves you in no doubt at all that it has taken place, not least because out of that one-off event flows an ever-present reality.

We've already mentioned David Pawson's analysis of the occasions in the New Testament when people are said to have been filled with the Spirit or 'baptized in Holy Spirit', and his conclusion that they, and any others who happened to have been around at the time, knew that it had happened because they had seen, or more usually heard, it happen. Pawson examines the language used in the Bible for this initial reception of the Spirit, including such terms as being baptized, drinking, being filled, having the Spirit fall upon, come upon or be poured out upon, being sealed and anointed, and he concludes that:

It is surely inconceivable that an event described in the language just examined could happen to a person without them or anyone else being aware of it! To claim that such terminology could be used where not even the person most affected was conscious of anything happening is to rob language of meaning and reduce it to the level of absurdity.[2]

He goes on to suggest that being baptized in the Spirit always overflows vocally, and that the gifts of speaking in tongues and/or prophecy are the most common evidence, although other outbursts of praise can also be present. Evangelicals who assert that you must have received the Spirit because you have believed in Jesus, and Catholics who think you must have received the Spirit because you have been baptized are both equally mistaken, according to Pawson. If you don't know you've received, and if that reception hasn't left you with something you didn't have before, you probably haven't!

The antidote to uncertainty

But what of those who are genuinely Christian, have received the Spirit through which they have been 'born again', but, like the Christians we studied from Acts 8 and 19, have never had anything supernatural happen to them? Am I going back on my argument that they have received the Spirit? No, I don't think I am, and I think I'd like to be a bit more moderate than Pawson. But I do think that part of the package, when the Spirit comes, is the gifts he brings with him, some of them clearly 'supernatural'. These gifts, as we have seen, are vital for mission and ministry in the life of the church, but according to the argument from John and Paul above, they are pretty useful for assurance, too. I'm not saying that anyone who doesn't feel certain of salvation isn't saved, but I do believe that through the Holy Spirit God intends to give us memorable and ongoing experience of things which simply couldn't happen without that Spirit. All the more reason, I believe, to make sure we unwrap all the presents.

So to hope that you might have received the Spirit, or to see the evidence for having received him only in terms of natural, general,

Christian niceness, is not much use when it comes to John's and Paul's attempts to convince you of your standing in Christ. Their readers would clearly have known the experience of being filled with the Spirit such that the arguments were totally convincing: if we have to ask how we know we've received, there's clearly something wrong!

So back to our question again: why should I be charismatic? Because, quite simply, a charismatic experience in the past and on-going charismatic spirituality now is meant to provide an antidote to uncertainty when it comes to your standing before God. I can speak in tongues whenever I like: that proves that I've received the Holy Spirit, and that in turn proves that God has saved me, is saving me and will save me. There's no condemnation for me, and I can know that I live in God and he in me, and that one day we will live together in heaven for ever. A massive outbreak of charismatic renewal could free the church from our grovelling, our uncertainty and our insecurity so that we could stop worrying and get on with the job in hand.

Chapter 7

Going by the Book

Why should I be charismatic? Because, I shall attempt to tell you in this chapter, obedience to the Bible demands it. I am making a huge assumption here, of course, but I think I can make it without too much controversy. That assumption is that as Christians we are seeking to live in obedience to the Bible. Even the most liberal of Christians, who might want to reinterpret huge chunks of it which they felt they couldn't cope with, would still say that they were seeking to live in obedience; that's exactly why the surgery was necessary, precisely to make it liveable by. So I'll take that for granted, and move on to ask whether or not the Bible does, in fact, tell us to be charismatic.

My argument here will be based on two sorts of evidence, which I shall call 'direct' and 'indirect'. We'll begin with the latter, then look at a direct command, and then return to some further indirect evidence.

The indirect evidence

We've already seen a couple of passages from the Old Testament which speak of the promise of God to his people that he would one day pour out his Spirit and create a new relationship, based not on outward ceremonies and observances but on inner spiritual reality. We know that in Jesus all God's promises have been or will be fulfilled, and we know that when Jesus burst on to the scene to be baptized by John in the River Jordan he was hailed as the one who would do inwardly with the Holy Spirit what John had been doing outwardly with water. We know finally that God's promise of the gift of the Holy Spirit was fulfilled on the day of Pentecost. God clearly intended his people to receive that gift of his Spirit, and in turn the gifts which the Spirit himself would give. So the question is this: why on earth should we not want to receive the Spirit? What does it say about our relationship with God if we are willing to withstand his purposes, reject his promises, and refuse his gifts? Now I will, of course, tackle the question of whether or not that which God promised looks anything at all like twenty-first-century charismatic renewal, but humour me for now. If God wanted, planned, predicted and delivered the gift of his Holy Spirit to all his people, what's the problem that we even need convincing that we should embrace it fully? Indirectly, the Bible assumes that all God's followers will want nothing but all his good gifts for them. What's the problem?

A direct command

But fortunately we're not left with that line of argument alone. Scripture doesn't just expect us to be filled with the Spirit: it directly commands it as well.

The clearest text, and the one on which I shall base the rest of this chapter, is Ephesians 5:18:

> Do not get drunk on wine, which leads to debauchery. Instead, *be filled with the Spirit.*

That ought to be clear enough and clinch the matter in itself, but we can't just pluck out isolated verses to prove points: we must look at the context, and examine the passage in which this verse sits and the gist of the author's argument. As we do so, we'll find the case strengthened even more.

The author, writing to a group of mostly Gentile Christians, urges them in 4:17, in the light of the theological truths which he has spelt out to them in the letter so far, to live no longer as the Gentiles do. In other words, they must no longer behave as they used to, and as those in the world around them still do. They must be different, and they must be seen to be different. He goes on to draw out several contrasts between the lifestyle they used to follow and that which they must now adopt as Christ's disciples. They must stop lying, and speak the truth (4:25), use their anger differently (4:26), work instead of stealing (4:28), give up immorality and obscenity (5:3–5), and so on. And, in addition, they must give up drunkenness, which leads to all kinds of debauchery, and be filled with the Spirit instead, which will lead to praise and worship (5:18–20). As I said, those five words, 'Be filled with the Spirit', ought to be enough on their own to convince us, but they do beg a couple of questions which we will have to examine quite closely before we arrive at what I believe is the only possible conclusion.

The first question is this: are those words, addressed originally to the first-century Ephesian church, still legally binding (as it were) on us? Clearly there are some commands in the Bible which we are perfectly at liberty to ignore, or at the very least reinterpret. All that stuff in the Old Testament about cutting up animals and calling in the priest if we find a bit of mildew on the wall clearly does not apply to us nowadays, or so most of us assume. It was for a time and a place, but has now been superseded. Similarly there is a command in the first three gospels to pay our taxes to Caesar: most of us would agree that what that really means for today is that we shouldn't fiddle our income tax, not that we should send a cheque off to Rome. The whole area of theology which deals with questions like these of the interpretation of the Bible is know as 'hermeneutics', and we'll come on to that in Chapter 9; meanwhile, the question 'Does Ephesians 5:18 apply to me today?' is certainly a valid question.

But we can answer it by asking another question: is there any reason why it might *not* apply to us? Most of the people reading this book are likely to be Gentile Christians who have come to Christ from a world where lying, stealing, immorality and all the rest of it is common currency. Have we any reason to suggest that the author would *not* want us to turn from that way of life to a holy lifestyle, one which pleases the Lord? It makes a lot of sense to regard the rest of chapters 4 and 5 as speaking to us: we would be unlikely to say, for example, that we are excluded from the author's command to get rid of bitterness, rage, anger, brawling, slander and malice (4:31). So why the problem with 5:18? In the absence of convincing proof that this injunction has passed away, we have to conclude that we too are commanded to 'be filled with the Spirit'.

The second question, though, is slightly more difficult. What does it mean to 'be filled with the Spirit'? What actually happens when I am, and how often do I have to be filled?

The second part is easy to answer, since in the Greek in which the New Testament was originally written there are two distinct tenses used for imperatives or commands. If you heard me say to my daughter 'Brush your teeth' I might be saying one of two things, and only the context and my tone of voice could enable you to distinguish between them. I might be telling her to get into the habit of regular teeth-brushing, morning and night every day of her life. Or alternatively, I might be telling her to get up those stairs and do it now! We can't hear the author's tone of voice, but fortunately that doesn't matter: we can tell by the way he spells it. What he is saying here is the former, not the latter: go on and on and on being filled with the Spirit. Make it a habit you practise, a lifestyle you embrace, in much the same way as you make a lifestyle of honesty and purity.

But that doesn't help with the first part of our question: what does being filled with the Spirit actually entail? Many people pray regularly that they might be filled with the Spirit, but if you were to ask them whether or not that prayer had been answered, they would be unable to tell you with any degree of conviction. How might we deal with this dilemma?

It is a general principle, and one which we have already seen worked out, that if we find something in the Bible which we don't understand it is often because the original readers knew something we don't. If I were writing a letter to someone, and I used the initials 'DBF' it would be a fairly safe bet that I was writing to an Anglican who already understood that term. But if in my letter I mentioned the DBF and went on to explain that this stood for the Diocesan Board of Finance, the committee in my Anglican diocese which was responsible for all matters to do with money, income and expenditure, you might guess that my letter was addressed to someone outside the Anglican jargon, for example a Baptist. The fact that in the first example I didn't bother to spell it out indicates clearly that I didn't think I needed to explain, since my reader would be perfectly well aware what I was going on about.

So when the author tells the recipients of his letter, without further explanation, to be filled with the Spirit, that can only be because they knew the experience perfectly well and didn't need it spelt out. Here we come back to what I said in an earlier chapter, that the first Christians would have known only too well what being filled with the Spirit entailed, since for them it would have been a living experience. They would have been baptized in the Spirit at their water-baptism service, and they would most likely have had ongoing experience of some of the Spirit's gifts, such as tongues or prophecy. In times of doubt this reality of the presence of the Spirit would remind them of the fact of their saving relationship with God and set them on an even keel again. So the author's instruction to them to be filled with the Spirit would be understood as a reminder that their experience of baptism in the Spirit was in need of continual topping up. In the famous words, they needed to be filled again and again because they leaked!

What would have happened when they were filled? Again, we perhaps don't know exactly if we've never experienced this kind of a filling, even after praying faithfully for God to fill us. But clearly something was meant to happen. We've already noted the fact that, in the New Testament, baptism in the Spirit was a visible and audible event, but the passage we're looking at takes us a little further. Throughout this section there are, as we mentioned, a series of contrasts. How do you talk to one another? Previously by lying, but now by telling the truth. How do you earn a crust? In the past, by stealing, but now by honest work. How do you treat others? No longer by giving them a kicking, but now with kindness and compassion. Is it too large a step of logic, therefore, to paraphrase verse 18 something like this: 'You used to get intoxicated on alcohol, which led you into all kinds of debauchery: now get intoxicated instead on the Spirit, which will lead you into praise'? The fact that this parallel is used suggests at least some similarity between the two different types of intoxication, and of course drunkenness was exactly the accusation levelled at the apostles on the day of Pentecost.

So be filled with the Spirit, says the author, in a way which is continuous with your initial baptism in the Spirit when you first believed. And – although this would seldom have applied in the early church – if you've not even heard of the Spirit then make sure that situation is remedied as soon as possible.

Living in obedience

Once we take this command as normative for New Testament Christianity, we can see that other passages in the Bible, while they may not *instruct* us to be filled with the Spirit quite as directly as Ephesians 5:18 does, nevertheless presuppose that an ongoing experiential encounter with the Spirit is part and parcel of what it means to live in obedience to Jesus. The most famous passages to deal with this are in 1 Corinthians 12 to 14: we're not specifically commanded to be filled, but the passages only work if they were written to those who were *already* filled and were perfectly aware of what that filling meant. This is on a par with Jesus teaching his disciples what we now call the 'Lord's Prayer': his words 'When you pray, say...' only make sense if spoken to those who did pray. He was not telling them to do it, but only telling them how to do it when they did. Many texts in the New Testament discuss what life in the Spirit entails and involves: the fact that we're seldom told as clearly as we are in Ephesians to be filled does not mean that it is a marginal command. On the contrary, the presence of those interpretative passages reinforces the expectation that reception of the Spirit is the natural birthright of every believer.

Some passages do take us further, though. We're told to pray in the Spirit (Ephesians 6:18; Jude 20), to live by the Spirit (Galatians 5:16,25; 1 Peter 4:6), eagerly to desire the gifts of the Spirit (1 Corinthians 14:1,5,39) and so on. Surely all of these instructions can only be meaningfully obeyed if we have fully received the Spirit and are constantly being refilled? To avoid the charismatic experience of baptism in the Spirit might just place us in danger of disobedience to many other scriptural injunctions. But conversely, an openness to and a seeking after the Spirit's fullness will enable us to live much more closely to biblical ideals. Dare we ignore this danger and this opportunity?

So what's the problem?

The problem, I suspect, is basically fear. When you think about it, fear is usually lurking behind most of our disobedience to scripture; that's why we're not very good at feeding the poor, turning the other cheek, sharing Jesus with our friends and family, giving money away, and all the thousand-and-one other little acts of disobedience which are part and parcel of our lives and which go unnoticed most of the time. And when we are challenged, we make up clever theologies to get ourselves off the hook. I can remember arguing long and hard with an otherwise very faithful and committed member of one of the churches I served in over the subject of tithing. I had gone to work in a church where the guiding principle was 'If we all muck in and give a little we'll have enough, and it won't hurt anyone too much.' I began unashamedly to preach tithing, and suggested that the biblical principle was that we all give a lot, and that it should hurt. As you might imagine, this went down like a lead balloon, but one man in particular just wouldn't let it go, and we argued endlessly (although in a very friendly manner) about whether someone living on a pension could afford 10 per cent, whether the income tax we pay to the government nowadays hadn't replaced the Old Testament principle of tithing, whether his giving to the cat's home or whatever should be included, and so on. It became very clear to me that he was simply trying to wriggle out of it, and mustering every kind of argument he could to do so. (They say the definition of repartee is what you would have said at the time if you'd thought of it: some years later a friend pointed out to me that the Old Testament command to tithe 10 per cent of your money is actually a better deal than in the New Testament, where Jesus goes for either 50 per cent – Luke 3:11, 19:8 – or 100 per cent – Mark 10:21!)

Exactly the same was true for me as I was struggling painfully towards charismatic renewal. I've already told you about my weekly visits to a charismatic church: from the very first time I saw them in action I knew that what I was seeing chimed in exactly with what I believed the New Testament church would have been like. As I listened to the Bible being preached week by week I was convinced of the truth of the message: what I was hearing was not some twisted propaganda, but the honest exposition of scripture in the power of the Holy Spirit. Yet I was terrified to let it all get too close to me. The bottom line was that I was (and still am to a high degree) a control freak, and there was no way I was going to start doing the things these charismatics were doing, even though I knew that what they were doing was thoroughly in line with the Bible. I really don't think there is any way you can read the New Testament honestly and believe that the authors are not writing about a charismatic church. I think with hindsight that I did have integrity in my struggles: I knew this was right and of God, but I also knew clearly that I was resisting him. I think he can probably cope with that, and is actually a lot more pleased with the honesty of that position than he is with our tortured theological wranglings which we use to get us off the hook but which don't actually fool anyone for very long. I believe he can work with me through my struggles much more effectively than he could if I had closed myself off to him with excuses.

But all this begs a deeper question: what kind of a God do we think we've got if we have to talk ourselves out of receiving his gifts for fear that they will in some way harm us? I realized after some years in parish ministry that the unarticulated fantasy of many Christians was that if they really did let down the barriers and allow God in closer his purpose would be in some way to upset them, violate them as people and do them harm. God was therefore someone from whom we had to protect ourselves, not someone whom we could trust and draw close to in intimacy. No-one ever said that, of course. They all knew in theory that he was kind, loving, gentle and all the rest of it. But they felt it. You could see it in their eyes, in their bodies, and in where they chose to sit in church!

This is not a new problem, and Jesus tackled it head on with his first followers. You lot are only human, right? Any of you got kids of your own? Would you deliberately give them something which would harm them if they asked you for something good? Slip a snake in their lunch box? Broken glass in their sandwiches? Well then, if you mere mortals can get it right, how much more will your Father in heaven, the perfect God himself, give only good things to those who ask him? That's Matthew's version of the incident (well, actually my paraphrase of Matthew's version). But Luke adds a twist: 'how much more will your Father in heaven give the *Holy Spirit* to those who ask him!' God isn't out to get us: he's out to bless us. Really he is!

There is one final matter at which we must look, the question of how we can know that what the Bible is describing is the same thing that we see today in the manifestations and practices of the charismatic movement. But since this is a major area, and in particular a major criticism which may be aimed at renewal, I have decided it warrants a chapter on its own, so having flagged up that question, I'll leave it for now and deal with it later.

So, once again, why should I be charismatic? Simply, I believe, because the Bible tells me I must, and expects that I will be. It's just not an option.

Chapter 8

Biblical Theology

I've already mentioned the fact that my first attempt at degree-level education came to an abrupt end when I failed my preliminary Chemistry exams at York and was politely asked to leave. This meant that when I returned to university to begin training for the ministry I couldn't get a grant for my first year. This was a terrible nuisance (although nowhere near as much of a nuisance as it is now having sons of my own who don't get grants at all, but just loans), and the upshot was that in order to survive my training I had no option but to live at home with my parents, which would be much cheaper than trying to move away. The only place within range where I could study theology was King's College, London, the very name of which struck terror into the hearts of evangelicals like me. King's in the 1970s was renowned for its liberal-critical approach to the Bible, and stories abounded in my circles of those who had gone there to study as good Bible-believing Christians and had emerged three years later as cynical and faithless wrecks. I longed to be able to escape to a nice safe college where my fundamentalist faith would be reinforced, but the finances simply would not let me.

So it was with great trepidation and much prayer back-up from friends that I arrived for my first day as a theological student at King's. Within a week I had fallen in love with the place, and I went on to spend three of the happiest years of my life there. My teachers turned out to be by and large sincere and godly men and women rather than the horned creatures from the pit I was expecting, and I took to the course material like a duck to water.

Or at least I thought I did. The reality was that I didn't hear a word anyone said to me. I could remember it, write essays on it and eventually pass exams on it, but I didn't really believe a word of it. I was an ex-Baptist, after all, and we knew our doctrine. Jesus came to earth to preach a Pauline gospel of justification by grace through faith, and woe betide anyone who told me any different.

So when my lecturers told me that Jesus came to bring in the kingdom of God, I humoured them and wrote the right kind of essays, but really I knew better. Jesus had come, so the story went, to defeat the evil reign of the Devil which had begun when Adam and Eve fell from grace, and to set free those who had been en-slaved and harmed by Satan's wiles. Every time Jesus healed sick people, or drove demons out of them, or took authority over the natural world, he did so in order to establish the rule, the kingship (or 'kingdom') of God and to drive back the forces of evil by one small step. Each healing encounter was one small battle within the great cosmic war, and every miraculous victory (or 'sign', as John calls them in his gospel) pointed to the fact that the kingdom of God was forcefully advancing. Very few of my teachers actually believed that Jesus *did* heal anyone or drive out any demons, or that there were any such people as Adam, Eve or Satan: that was simply the mythology of which the Bible is a write-up. Any great teacher naturally attracted to himself all sorts of myths and legends, and Jesus was no exception. But if he had done all those sorts of things, that was what it would have meant.

Theory and practice

Then, of course, we had to study the works of the great theologians of our time. We were told to read Albert Schweitzer's seminal book *The Quest of the Historical Jesus*,[1] in which he insisted that in order fully to understand Jesus we must see him in the context of his own worldview rather than ours. We must see him against the backdrop of first-century Jewish Apocalyptic, because everyone in Jesus' time expected the imminent inbreaking of God to wind up history, turn the moon to blood, smash up all Israel's enemies, and reign over the Jews in a new and perfect age-to-come. Given that set of expectations, Schweitzer said that Jesus spent his life in pursuit of a kingdom which never came, until he died a broken and disappointed man.

Next we had to read C.H. Dodd, who wrote about 'realized eschatology',[2] the belief that the kingdom had indeed come with Jesus, and that God's rule had begun. Jesus was not simply a frustrated wannabee Messiah, as Schweitzer believed, but rather the powerful inaugurater of a new world order. Not everyone agreed with Dodd, though: others pointed to the fact that the Bible talks about the kingdom as a future promise rather than a present reality. And then we had to read Oscar Cullmann, who in his *Christ and Time*[3] solved this dilemma neatly by introducing the concept of 'eschatological tension': the kingdom had indeed broken in with the ministry of Jesus, but had not been fully consummated, and would not be until his return in glory. The kingdom is here, but not yet here; the dawn has broken but the sun has not yet risen. We can't see it above the horizon, but we can see the light it is beginning to shed. This means that now we live in a kind of overlap time between the first and second comings of Jesus; we see some of the power of the kingdom but not all of it. The technical term for this waiting period is 'the end times', by the way, so next time some enthusiastic charismatic tells you we're living in the end times, you can reply, 'Yes, I know, and we have been for the last two thousand years!'

The more we learnt about these world-class theologians, the more fascinated I became, although on another level I still didn't hear what any of them were saying. The fact was, I can now understand with the wonderful gift of hindsight that no-one who had studied or taught New Testament theology – not Schweitzer, nor Dodd, nor Cullmann, nor my professors, nor even I myself – had ever seemed to stop to ask the question '*Well, where is it then?*' Where exactly is this kingdom which Jesus supposedly came to bring? Where are the healings, the miracles, the deliverances from evil spirits, the raisings from death? If the kingdom is here, even just a little bit of it, shouldn't we see some of it in action? We were treating the Bible as no more than a piece of interesting literature. Some of us did that because of our modernist liberal mindset which made us believe that there was simply no such thing as the supernatural, and that those who wrote about it were sincere but sadly misguided. Others, like me, didn't hear what the Bible actually said because we thought we already knew and so filtered out anything we heard which was different.

Well, I continued to write my essays, finally passed my degree, even went on to do some post-graduate research, and was duly ordained into the Church of England ministry. It was towards the end of my first curacy that I began to feel dry and frustrated. I was becoming more and more aware of the gulf between what the Bible suggested the church should be like and what my parish really was like. In particular I was getting sick of *telling* people who were not yet believers about God, when really I longed to be able to *show* them God in action.

Signs and wonders

In 1983 we went, as was our custom, to Spring Harvest, and it was one of those years when only one message penetrated my brain, coming from just about every speaker at every seminar I went to: it's no good just telling people about God if we can't show them God in action. I went home at the end of the week even more frustrated, but God had done his work: when after a few months of stewing I first heard about the ministry of John Wimber and a visit he would be making to London later in the year, I was ready! John, the blurb told us, had developed his 'Signs and Wonders' course out of the discovery that evangelism worked better when we didn't just tell people about God, but could show them God in action.

So one morning I got up at 3.30, drove into Norwich to get the coach to Victoria, and arrived in time for a day conference at Holy Trinity, Brompton, at which John was to set out his wares. I finally arrived back in Norwich at 2 a.m. the next day a changed (and thoroughly exhausted) person.

John had begun by teaching a theology of the kingdom of God. What he had said was almost word-for-word what my teachers at King's had taught me eight years earlier. Every bell within me began to ring as I heard my lectures replayed: Jesus came into a worldview of first-century Jewish Apocalyptic to proclaim and institute the rule or reign of God, he went round undoing the harm that Satan had done to people by inflicting them with disease, disharmony and dysfunctionality, and every miraculous act was a further step forward for the kingdom of God as it drove back the kingdom of darkness. But the kingdom which he inaugurated would not come fully until his return, so in the meantime we had to do the works of Jesus but with defeat as well as victory, failure as well as success. I listened enthralled as my New Testament lectures from King's were replayed, except that this time it was different. As John stopped teaching he stood us all up, and then invited the Holy Spirit to come and bring in some more of the kingdom now. During the next half an hour or so I watched enthralled as people received prayer for healing, as demons were expelled, as people received gifts of the Spirit for the first time, all accompanied with such a sense of the presence of God and such powerful manifestations of the Spirit. I wasn't the slightest bit scared; I was just overwhelmed with a sense of joy at seeing theology and practice coming together in such a powerful way.

This next step in my charismatic pilgrimage was purely an intellectual one: I embraced the teaching of John Wimber gladly and enthusiastically simply because it made such good theological sense, and because it allowed me to integrate the study of theology I had loved so much at King's with real-life charismatic experience. But it didn't remain intellectual for long: I signed up for the first large-scale British Vineyard conference at Westminster Central Hall, and spent a week finding out more about this remarkable man and his teaching. I returned to my parish all fired up and raring to go.

John had taught us that in his experience it took about a year to get healing ministry flowing. He told of the fact that in his experience, and that of many others, you had to pray for people for about a year and see nothing whatsoever happen, until one day breakthrough would come and people would start getting healed.[4] I was determined to get started as soon as possible, on the basis that the sooner we got going, the sooner the year would be up and we'd start seeing things happen.

So I began the next Sunday evening. I was not quite as bold as a friend who was also at the conference, who invited the Holy Spirit to come during a wedding he was taking on the Saturday, but Sunday evening wasn't too bad, I felt. I taught about John Wimber, his message and his ministry, and then I invited any who wanted prayer for healing to stand. I went along the row of eleven people with a friend who had been at the conference with me, praying for them out of sheer duty and with no expectation at all that anything would happen. We were amazed when nine out of the eleven received some kind of healing. I have no idea why I am better at this than John Wimber, but we kept going joyfully, seeing people's lives transformed as we began regularly to offer prayer ministry. But best of all, in a deep and secret place in my heart, was an overwhelming joy that what we were seeing was what Dodd and Cullmann and the others had only theologized about.

Why should I be charismatic? Because charismatic renewal represents, I believe, the actualization of the best of biblical theology. Academic theologians have a bad press in much of the church. I remember once hearing someone at a charismatic gathering say, 'We don't want any theology around here, we just want to be open to the Spirit!' While such a comment is profoundly silly, and is in fact in itself a theological statement, we do know what he meant. At its worst, academic study of the Bible can be dry, dusty, esoteric and totally divorced from church life. It may indeed set out to destroy what it regards as the simplistic faith of naïve 'fundamentalist' Christians, and can so easily knock down faith rather than building it up. But what I found so gut-wrenchingly powerful about John Wimber's ministry was that he took the best of biblical theology and then made it come alive before our very eyes. What theologians in the past had studied but never known in reality was now normative practice once again in the church. Schweitzer and the rest were sincere and did the best job they could, but they simply lived at the wrong time, before modernism and anti-supernaturalism had crumbled as belief systems. Their presuppositions prevented them from asking that logical next question to their theologizing, 'Where is the present reality of all this?'

For me, that tie-up between my formal theological education and my current charismatic practice is vital. I can't live with the kind of schizophrenia by which clergy write off their training for ministry as irrelevant or worse. I need to know that what I'm doing in the church is rooted in the Bible and in the best of thinking about it. In charismatic renewal the greatest biblical theology has once again become normative church practice: for me, being charismatic has a ring of truth and a sense of completeness about it. We can have our cake and eat it: we can have theology (and indeed very good theology) *and* be open to the Spirit. I reckon that to exist with only one or the other is to do ourselves, and the church of Jesus Christ, unacceptably down.

Chapter 9
....

Open to Interpretation

Why should I be charismatic? Because, I am going to argue in this chapter, it will help you to get the Bible right. We've talked about obeying the Bible, and about the theology of the Bible, but this is slightly different. We need the power of the Holy Spirit, I believe, if we are to understand and use the Bible correctly. We're going to need to get a bit technical at one or two points, I'm afraid, and you're going to have to learn a bit of German before we're finished, but this is an important issue, so grit your teeth and I'll try to make it as painless as I can for you (I hate it when my dentist says that: it always means I'm in for twenty minutes of agony). And just think how relieved you'll feel when it's over!

The roots of understanding

Let me begin with an important technical word: 'hermeneutics'. It comes from the Greek word for 'interpretation', and it refers to the branch of theology which deals with questions of how we understand the Bible today. Immediately you can see that it is a vital field, and fortunately some people enjoy it and so can help the rest of us.

Let's begin with a hermeneutical problem, just to get you in the mood and illustrate the problems. We'll do Ephesians 5:18 again, since it provides an excellent but fairly straightforward hermeneutical problem. 'Do not get drunk on wine,' the Bible says, and this is a fairly black-and-white issue. If I do get drunk on wine I'm disobeying scripture, and if I don't I'm not.

But what if I get drunk on Stella Artois? Or Captain Morgan, or Laphroaig, or Newcastle Brown? And, to complicate things even more, what if I get stoned smoking ganja? Am I disobeying the Bible then? One possible (though you may feel unconvincing) answer is to say that the Bible nowhere prohibits us from the excessive consumption of Laphroaig. In fact, try as I might, I can't find in my concordance any mention of Laphroaig at all, nor of ganja for that matter. So it must be OK.

The other view, though, and this is where the hermeneutics comes into play, is that what the author really meant was 'Don't get intoxicated on alcohol'. Therefore *any* beer, wine or spirit is included, whether or not the church in Ephesus in those days could obtain it from their local Oddbins. But what about smoking a spliff? There's no alcohol at all in marijuana as far as I know. So is that OK, then? No, because what the author really really meant was 'Don't get out of control on intoxicating substances of any nature', although he didn't know he meant that since he didn't have quite the illegal drugs problem that we have nowadays.

As soon as we start interpreting what the author of a biblical passage *actually* said and deciding what he *really* meant, we are engaging in hermeneutics, and you can see what a highly dangerous area it is to wander into. After all, we nearly legalized cannabis a couple of sentences ago! So when the character from the Monty Python film mishears a part of the Sermon on the Mount as 'Blessed are the cheesemakers', and his friend says that we must surely broaden that out to include all manufacturers of dairy products, they are engaging in a bit of tongue-in-cheek hermeneutics.

Clearly this is a most important branch of theology. If, as we decided in the last chapter, all Christians ought to be committed to living in obedience to the Bible, it is vital that we understand what the Bible actually says and what it means so that we can obey it accurately. Questions of morality, war and pacifism, crime and punishment, sex and relationships, money and poverty all hang on how we interpret the biblical texts which deal with those issues, or, as we saw in our foray above, how we interpret texts which don't deal with them except by implication. Many areas are, of course, trivial: if a woman goes to church without her hat on or if her husband wears a poly-cotton shirt, they are both engaging in hermeneutics, since they are disobeying two clear commands of scripture which they have decided (or probably their church culture has decided for them) do not apply to them. But does that mean that we are free to dispense with some other bits we would like not to apply to us?

The greatest danger in all this, you see, is that we use hermeneutics to grind axes. In Southern California, where the divorce rate is over 50 per cent and serial monogamy is the order of the day, some of Jesus' strictures on divorce and adultery are played down considerably by the church. Apartheid in South Africa came from an interpretation of biblical texts which conveniently allowed the rich white overlords to continue to oppress their black servants. Currently there is huge debate over whether it is OK to live in gay relationships or not. All these issues, and many more, seem from a cursory reading of the Bible to be clear-cut in the extreme, but those who want the Bible to say something different so that they can continue in their current lifestyle are working hard at playing the hermeneutics game – to prove, for example, that when it says in Leviticus 18:22 that God says 'Do not lie with a man as one lies with a woman; that is detestable', what God *really* means is 'To lie with a man as one lies with a woman is fine by me.' And when you think about it, how is that different from interpreting Leviticus 19:19 to mean that poly-cotton shirts are not a problem?

It's not just about personal morality or sartorial elegance either. Most of the arguments between different branches of the church are over this kind of issue. At what age should you baptize people? How much water should you use? Should you call your church leaders 'priests' or even 'Father'? Should we expect Jesus still to baptize people in the Holy Spirit? When? At their conversion, or at some time later? Churches have split over hermeneutical questions. It's not that those on one side are seeking to follow the Bible while the others aren't. They're both trying to follow the Bible *as they understand it*, and there precisely is the problem. In most churches it isn't the Bible which rules, but the interpreter of the Bible. There's a world of difference.

That's why we need theologians who specialize in this field to discover what the rules of hermeneutics are, so that they can say to us, 'I'm sorry but there is no way that the biblical text can be twisted around to mean *that*. There are rules to this game, and you've just broken them!'

So what has all this got to do with the issue in hand? Partly it has to do with the question I threw in above: what exactly does the Bible teach us to expect with regard to the Holy Spirit? I've tried to deal with that as we went along, and to forestall some of the hermeneutical questions, but there are clearly those in the church who would want to disagree with just about everything I've said, not because they don't believe in or value the Bible, but because their reading of the biblical texts is different from mine. I'll need to take them on a bit in Part III, so I won't stop to discuss those questions now, but I do want to look at the subject of hermeneutics from a slightly different point of view: it is my conviction that being filled with the Spirit and entering the world of charismatic renewal means that you do your hermeneutics in a very different way. It is this difference I want to explore.

Knowing the truth

The question which will lead us into this discussion can be framed like this: how does the Bible speak to us today? How exactly does the truth written up in the text get into our heads and begin to change our lives?

The classical view on this, a view held by many faithful, Bible-committed Christians, is that the truth is there and it just comes and gets us. We come as it were naked to the words on the page, and they yield up the full harvest of what God has to say to us. A famous German theologian called Rudolph Bultmann, who lived early last century, named this view 'presuppositionless exegesis'. He also said it was a total impossibility.

You cannot possibly, says Bultmann, approach a text without bringing some kind of presuppositions with you. The world you live in, the culture all around you, the church you have found a home in, your current circumstances and mood, Christian leaders and Bible teachers who have been influential for you: all these factors and many more besides will affect how you approach a text, and what you see in it. To take a trivial example, how do you feel as you read the text of Revelation 22:14–15?

> Blessed are those who wash their robes, that they may have the right to the tree of life and may go through the gates into the city. Outside are the dogs, those who practise magic arts, the sexually immoral, the murderers, the idolaters and everyone who loves and practises falsehood.

In particular, what about the dogs? A friend of mine used to hate that verse, because it told her that her beloved Labrador wouldn't go to heaven with her. My view, on the contrary, was one of relief that at least the afterlife will be free from smelly slobbery creatures who leave hairs all over your car seats, scare you with their growling and deposit little beanos on the golden pavements. My friend came to the text as a dog-lover, and it was to her a sad text; my reaction was somewhat different because my past experience of dogs, the conditioning from my parents and the fact that I just don't choose to spend my limited financial resources on hundreds of tins of 'Mankey Lumps with Liver, Beetroot and Crunchy Bits' had all conspired to help me view the text positively. Of course, a real hermeneutician would tell me that the verse has nothing whatsoever to do with canine immortality, but I use it to illustrate the point that to expect to come to the text without any presuppositions or feelings is to expect the impossible. What we expect to find or hope to find will tend to be what we do find.

We had an amusing example of this triumph of presuppositions over plain sense when we were away one week and our young daughter was visiting a Sunday School in a Baptist church. She emerged at the end of the service waving the statutory picture she'd coloured and cardboard *thing* she'd made, and told us that in her story Jesus had gone to a wedding. 'That's nice,' we commented. 'And did anything happen while he was there?' 'Yes', Vicki replied. 'They ran out of drink, so Jesus turned some water into juice!' The church's teetotal stance and the desire not to corrupt vulnerable young minds with the evil ways of the world had brought about a reinterpretation of the plain sense of the text.

So if we always come to the text with our presuppositions, there is an implication which follows, which to many Christians is scary in the extreme. We're often told that scripture alone must be our guide in life, our source of truth and our way of receiving God's revelation to us. But in fact what we're saying is that it isn't scripture alone, but scripture plus the way we view it, due to our background and circumstances. And so the next question is this: which comes first, scripture or experience? To say that scripture does is naïve, but to say that experience does is highly dangerous and subjective. It's as if we could make the Bible say anything we wanted it to, just as you could make a sundial tell you it was any time you liked by walking around it at night with a powerful torch. So what exactly is the relationship between the Bible and our experience, and how can we get out of this place between the Devil and the deep blue sea?

The impact of experience

Two German theologians called Fuchs and Ebeling, who were responsible for a move forward known as the 'New Hermeneutik',[1] can help us here. They agreed with Bultmann about the impossibility of 'presuppositionless exegesis' and claimed that whenever we come to the Bible we bring with us a *vorverstandnis* or 'preunderstanding' of what the text will mean. But if the text is to speak to us in some way, we must have some kind of *einverstandnis* with it, a kind of common understanding of its world, some shared horizons or empathy. Without *einverstandnis* we will simply not hear what the text is saying.

Let me help all this clever German make sense to you with a story. We were on holiday, and went on the Sunday morning to the little village church near where we were staying. The vicar preached a sermon on Jesus healing a blind man, and he made a good job of it, bringing the story alive and expounding the text with clarity and interest. Then the time drew near for the application of this story to our daily lives. 'Therefore,' proclaimed the preacher, 'we too, like Jesus, must be kind to blind people, by helping them across the road.'

Now I would have believed that sermon: I might even have preached something like it, except for one thing: I had just returned from a conference during the course of which I had been part of a group praying for a lady to get her sight back, a prayer which, by the grace of God, had been answered. That *experience* had altered the way I understood the text: no longer could it simply be talking about helping blind people across the road. Helping people across the road is, of course, a good thing to do (always assuming they want to go), but the text said so much more, which before my experience I would have missed.

You see, before that conference my preunderstanding (to go back to Fuchs and Ebeling) of Mark 10 was that healings like that didn't happen for me. I'd never done anything like that, so I had nowhere to put that story. Jesus did do it, I had no doubt, but I don't, so I had no empathy or common horizons with the text. In German translation, my *vorverstandnis* was negative, and I had no *einverstandnis*. But the experience of actually seeing someone blind healed flipped everything over through 180 degrees. Suddenly my *vorverstandnis* became positive: healing blind people was possible today: I knew because I'd seen it! Suddenly I established some *einverstandnis*: Jesus saw blind people healed; so could I! We do live in the same world after all! This mental flip dramatically changed the way I viewed the story in the Bible: the application could now become 'we should all be kind to blind people by praying for them to get their sight back'! I had read that passage many times over the previous thirty-odd years and never once had it occurred to me that I might try to do what Jesus had done. I had simply filtered it out because it was meaningless to me. But an experience had changed all that.

Now, to a good conservative evangelical like me this was an alarming heresy. I had always been taught that scripture must come first and dictate experience, but now I had found that it had worked exactly the other way round. Imagine my distress, but imagine also my relief when I discovered that this was not a private heresy which Rudolph Bultmann and I shared, but was rather the whole way in which the Bible was written. The more I thought about it, the more I came to believe the disturbing yet liberating truth that scripture alone was not enough.

When scripture is not enough

It's Acts 15. The early church is in council. Disturbing reports have reached the leadership, and things need Sorting Out. Peter has been caught baptizing Gentiles without first making them become Jewish. Gentiles in the church? Shock, horror. The scriptures are God's gift to *his* people the Jews, not for every Tom, Dick or Harry. The Messiah came to the Chosen Race. When it came to Gentile Christians, the church's *vorverstandnis* was 'No way!' But then Peter tells of an experience he had back in chapter 10, when in the middle of his sermon God quite suddenly and without so much as a by-your-leave poured out his Spirit on the Gentiles, just as he had done on some Jews on the day of Pentecost. Paul and Barnabas throw in their two-pennorth and tell of some of the similar experiences they've had working with Gentiles. There doesn't seem to be too much doubt that God really is at work here, but what are we to make of it?

The clincher comes when James pipes up. We've heard what God is actually doing, he says, and guess what? I've found it in the Bible! He reads a couple of verses from Amos 9, verses which each of them must have read hundreds of times before, but this time he can see more in them. God really is interested in calling both Jews and Gentiles. Then James says something fascinating: 'The words of the Prophets are in agreement with this.' Experience has come first, and the scriptures agree with it. I would have wanted to make sure that my experience agreed with scripture, but no, it's the other way round entirely. The council finds that its *vorverstandnis* and its *einverstandnis* have done a flip, and suddenly the church becomes universal. Gentiles are welcome without first going through circumcision, a decision for which I and approximately 50 per cent of Gentile Christians are very grateful. But the scriptures alone had not led them to this decision. Amos' words had always been there for centuries, but no-one had noticed or thought to apply them to this issue.

Two more examples will drive this point home. The book of Nehemiah describes an occasion when the people assembled to hear the Law being read. The words and the laws they encapsulated would not have been unfamiliar, but on this occasion there was an added ingredient. Something which we would probably now recognize as the conviction of the Holy Spirit swept across that town square, and the people began mourning and weeping, suddenly aware of their sinfulness. This experience led to a mass gathering three weeks later for confession, prayer and fasting. It wasn't that the words of the Law hadn't been there before, or that the people had been on a sinning-spree any more than usual. Once again, as in Acts 10, a sovereign in-breaking of the Spirit of God had opened their eyes to what had been in the scriptures all along, but which they'd never really noticed before. Scripture, once again, was not enough by itself.

This time we're in Luke 24, walking along the road with some deeply disappointed disciples. There is such deep pathos in the phrase 'we had hoped' in verse 21, words which resonate down the years with all the deepest disappointments of the human race. The stranger whom they had met on the road begins to explain the scriptures to them, telling them everything there which concerned the Messiah, the necessity of his death and the certainty of his resurrection. But guess what? The scriptures were not enough! They still didn't get it! Why? Because, as we're told in verse 16, they were somehow kept from recognizing him. But then comes an experience: the stranger sits down to eat with them, breaks bread and vanishes. Their eyes are opened: suddenly it all comes clear. They thought back to their conversation, and realized with the benefit of hindsight that something had been going on for them. But the scriptures only made sense once the supernatural concealment had become supernatural revelation. The experience of sitting at the table with Jesus had flipped their *einverstandnis*.

'Where does the Bible say that?'

Now you may be asking by now what on earth this has got to do with charismatic spirituality, and how it contributes in any way towards an answer to the question 'Why should I be charismatic?' The answer, I believe, is that while this hermeneutical method works, in fact, for everyone, not all of us want to accept that this is how it is. Charismatics, it seems to me, are the most comfortable with it, and it is this fact which brings them under some of the sharpest attacks from others. We'll look at some of those attacks later, but in a nutshell the issue is this: are we allowed to do stuff before we can prove conclusively from the Bible that it's OK to do it?

A few years ago there was an outbreak of activity in a church in Canada which became known as the 'Toronto Blessing'. During times of prayer and ministry people would behave in some strange ways, including falling over, laughing like drains, twitching or vibrating, or making strange sounds which some felt were reminiscent of animal noises. Some people jumped at it, flying half-way round the world to catch some of this blessing; others were slightly cautious, and went along just to see how it felt; but others decried and denounced the whole thing as a creation of disturbed humans or, even worse, as a demonic deception. The big cry of the critics was 'Where can you find *that* in the Bible?' and the presupposition behind the cry was that they ought to have been able to do so. Now just suppose for one minute that the Toronto Blessing was indeed a genuine manifestation of the Holy Spirit of God (a view which I happen to take, but that's not important right now). Can you see how dangerous it might have been for those who stood at a distance and criticized, and who therefore not only missed out on something which God had for them but also probably influenced others away from it too? If that kind of attitude had won the day in Acts 15, there would still be no Gentiles in the church. 'Where does it say in the scriptures that God is going to give his Spirit to the Gentiles and make them speak in tongues?' you can hear them asking. So often, you see, the question, 'Where does it say that in the Bible?' is not really a genuine, searching question, but a nasty statement which means 'I cannot believe for one minute that you can find that in the Bible, so don't even try!' Once again, presuppositions rule.

Now, of course, there is an equal and opposite danger: the whole Toronto thing might indeed have been a demonic deception. The problem with this 'suck it and see' approach to religious experience is that it is risky. So far better, the cautious reply, to hedge our bets and stay on the safe side. Let's make sure *before* we try anything that it is truly biblically kosher. This is certainly a less risky approach, at least on the surface, but then there is always the risk that we might miss out on something because we can't find it in the Bible although it is there really. Our negative presuppositions might have blinded us totally to it, and without risking the experience we'll never have our eyes opened. So in fact it's risky either way.

Charismatic spirituality tends towards the approach which says 'Let's give this a go!' Charismatics are less frightened of risking it, because they trust their powers of discernment and are convinced that if they do get into something which is less than God's best for them, he is perfectly capable of warning them off, as long as their hearts remain set on a desire to follow him and walk with him. There obviously are casualties, those who have gone astray into serious error, but then so there are on the other side of the camp. It is much more publicly visible to stray off into definite error, but is that any worse a sin than the slightly more hidden closedness to the work of the Holy Spirit, into which many more cautious Christians are forced?

My conviction is that to shut ourselves off from the possibility of God leading us anywhere new is on balance more of a danger than to embrace with joy new experiences from the Spirit. And of course, at the end of the day being a Christian is not simply about following a set of rules from a book: it is about growing in a relationship with Jesus to the point where we begin to know instinctively what will or will not please him. Look at Ephesians 5 again, where in verse 10 we're told to 'find out what pleases the Lord'. The Bible is there to help us do that, but it is not the only way. Our prayer-life, our whole spirituality in fact, is about growing in this knowledge of the one whom we love and serve.

So why should I be charismatic? Because it seems to be the case that to open ourselves up to the Spirit also opens us up to new experiences and therefore new insights into the Bible and into God himself. This ties in with the 'Play' characteristic we mentioned earlier: for the charismatic it's OK to enjoy being a Christian, and a paranoid or neurotic scanning of the text of the Bible before we're allowed to do anything is surely less than the freedom for which Christ has set us free. It is part of the work of the Spirit to make Jesus real to us: to close ourselves off to that work is like reducing a marriage relationship to reading your partner's biography instead of making love to them. And, of course, it is also part of the Spirit's work to lead us into all the truth: why should we settle for less than that, and concentrate only on those bits of the Bible which our experience so far has opened us up to?

Part Three
. . . .
Any Objections?

Chapter 10

A Very Horrid Thing?

I have tried to convince you so far that charismatic spirituality is a good, right and biblical thing which should be embraced by all right-thinking Christians, and only you will know whether or not I have done a good job. But in this next section I want to move on in an attempt to take seriously some of the many criticisms which have been levelled at charismatics, and enter into a defence of renewal not on my terms but on those of its opponents.

And opponents it has, sometimes very vehement opponents indeed. How people can be so hostile towards a move of God which gives the church new life and vitality, which, as we shall see, helps it grow and fulfil Christ's commission to us, which helps it keep youngsters instead of losing them, and above all which is so clearly biblical, is a question which needs a serious answer, and my hope is that I can at least have a go at doing it justice, having listened as carefully as I can to renewal's critics.

Can we still expect the Spirit's power today?

The first and most crucial question we will need to look at has to do with the expectation that we can still experience today the gifts of the Spirit which we read about in the Bible (or something which we assume to be very much like them). Bishop Butler is reported to have said to John Wesley, after he began to experience the gifts and power of the Spirit, 'Sir, the pretending to extraordinary revelations and gifts of the Holy Ghost is a horrid thing, a very horrid thing!'[1]

How can we be sure that God intended the power of the Spirit for us today, and that we are not simply making it all up? To keep it simple, there are three main views on this question. Let's examine them in turn.

The 'Liberal' view is that they didn't happen then and they don't happen now. The stories we read in the Bible are mythical accounts of what people thought prophets and Messiahs *ought* to do, but we cannot seriously believe that they are actual historical fact. No doubt there were some great prophets and teachers around, but you know what it's like; stories grow up around them, and they get embroidered over the years, and before you know it you've got miracle workers. When I was younger (quite a bit younger, as it goes) I genuinely and wholeheartedly believed that Jimi Hendrix came from another planet, because no mere human could play guitar like that! This is the stuff, claim the Liberals, that miracles are made of. Stupid and gullible people begin to believe the most outrageous things, and before you know where you are, you have a full-blown supernaturalism and a crowd of followers believing it. Therefore to claim that the Spirit gives gifts like tongues, prophecy or healing today is as daft as claiming that he ever did.

The 'Cessationist' view says that they did happen then but they don't happen now. We shouldn't expect to see any gifts of the Spirit, or at least not any 'supernatural' ones today, because they were only ever intended for the first stage in the church's life. When you're building a house you need, in the early stages, to put up some scaffolding round it to help the building process. But once the building is finished the scaffolding is taken away and the house stands in its own right. Or when you get into your car on a cold morning you need to operate the choke (or nowadays it is operated automatically for you) to get the motor running. But once you're warmed up, the choke goes in and you forget about it. The gifts of the Spirit are like that, claim the Cessationists. The church needed them to get going, but they were then withdrawn by God once things were up and running and the Bible was written to tell us all we need to know once and for all.

The 'Pentecostal/charismatic' view says that they did happen then and they do happen now. We can trust the biblical evidence about the supernatural work of the Spirit, and since there is no apparent expectation in the Bible that they were only for the first century or so, we are perfectly right in claiming that they still happen today. We may not be able to prove conclusively that what charismatics do nowadays is exactly the same as people did in the first century (although I shall attempt to do so in the next chapter) but we can make a pretty fair guess that it's as close as makes no odds. So we should take literally biblical instructions, such as that in Ephesians 5:18 which we've already mentioned, to be filled with the Spirit, and expect that God will answer our prayers in unmistakable ways.

These three views, then, are three different attempts to deal with questions as to the possibility of the power of the Spirit being in evidence in the church today. It won't surprise you to learn that I am a subscriber to the third; I hope you'd picked that up by now! But the other two do need some examination, not least because of their popularity in some sections of the church.

The Liberal view

The Liberal view is, as we have already noted, a product of modernism. As scientists grew in their skill in the seventeenth century, there was less and less of a need for 'God' to explain things – science could do that perfectly well, or was at least on the way to doing so. The universe was seen as a giant machine, the different parts of which moved in pre-determined ways according to built-in laws or principles, and a God who interfered with it in 'supernatural' or miraculous ways was simply unthinkable. Rather, the divine genius lay in the power of God to set it all up in the first place, and to design the 'laws' by which it would run. Miracles were not just impossible, they were unnecessary. The parts of life which could not be dealt with by the scientists, such as 'religion' or 'faith', came to be relegated to a slightly inferior world not that far removed from 'superstition'. People's faith became more and more privatized and separated off from the 'real' world of everyday life, where science was god.

Then, of course, the hungry scientists, looking for ever more areas upon which to experiment, inevitably turned their attention to this strange but persistent phenomenon called 'religion' and began to ask scientific questions about it. The science of 'Biblical Criticism' was born in the late nineteenth century, as scientific method began to be applied to the Bible, and later scientists began to examine so-called 'spiritual experiences' in terms of the emerging field of psychology.

Now I am not denying that there was any usefulness in these areas of study – the benefits have been tremendous in helping thoughtful Christians understand their faith more fully – but the problem is that so many of those applying scientific method to matters of faith begin with the presuppositions which modernist culture and its metanarrative (that only the concrete and physical is real) tells them. I am quite happy to know that when I pray certain wave-patterns are set up in my brain: the problems come when people try to tell me that prayer is *nothing more than* a set of brain-wave patterns. The modernist culture found it self-evidently obvious that the supernatural wasn't real, and so the Liberal theology which is based on it has no option but to deny the miraculous in any way, shape or form, either then or now.

The problem for this view in a new millennium is that people just don't believe it any more. We've already talked about this shift, and noted that both academics and the man in the street have begun to abandon modernism. The important point is that we're realizing that not only is it not true any more; it never was true. Modernism was a false path which led to a dead end, and more and more people are rejecting its dogmas in the light of the emptiness which it has brought to us (and indeed to our churches) and the increasing amount of evidence to the contrary. Modernism is not totally defunct, of course, and still has its outposts in some obscure corners of academia, but it is failing fast, and the amazing search for 'spirituality', particularly among the young, is evidence enough of its bankruptcy. The Liberal view just doesn't hold water any more and will, I believe, be abandoned totally within a generation, although the damage it has done to the churches will take much longer to heal.

The Cessationist view

But what then of the Cessationist view? Unlike the Liberals, the Cessationists do at least believe in the possibility of the supernatural: they just don't believe we should expect it today. On what evidence do they base this assumption?

The Cessationist view reached its height, and its clearest expression, in the writings of one Benjamin Warfield, who lived from 1855 to 1921 and was for a time professor of theology at Princeton Seminary in America. His most famous book, *Counterfeit Miracles*, was published in 1918.[2] In it he states what was to become the classic Cessationist position, that the gifts of the Spirit were given to the Apostles only, to validate their position and to launch the early church. After the original Apostles had all died, the gifts were withdrawn as no longer necessary.

A similar view was propounded by John Darby, who carved world history up into a series of different eras or 'dispensations', and stated that God dealt with people in different ways during the different dispensations. The gifts of the Spirit were for one particular dispensation, but were never intended to be permanent possessions of the church. Darby's views were widely disseminated via the *Schofield Reference Bible*, in which the text of the Authorized Version was annotated with dispensationalist comments and doctrine.

It can be illuminating to ask any theologian where they are coming from. What factors might have influenced their thought? Warfield, we know, lovingly and devotedly nursed a chronically sick wife for many years until her death: we can only guess what impact this situation had on him, and in particular on his views about healing. But apart from that, we know that he was fighting on two fronts at once, and trying to keep at bay two very different threats to his strict Calvinism. The first was the encroaching tide of the Liberal views which we have outlined above. As a conservative evangelical, Warfield was alarmed by any attack on the authenticity of the Bible, and so he was fighting hard to say that the biblical records of the miraculous were totally accurate and to be believed. But he was also facing the growth of Pentecostalism, and increasing numbers of claims that the very things which had happened in the Bible were once again in evidence today. This too was dangerous to his high commitment to scripture, because if the written Word was God's final and complete revelation to us, we could not possibly believe in any further revelation, such as might come through tongues or prophecy. Any such 'further' revelation must by definition be 'adding' to what was the full and complete revelation in the Bible, and so must necessarily be wrong and evil. This false step of logic, which we will explore in a later chapter, is what drove Warfield's work; and this dual emphasis, that miracles did happen then but cannot happen now, is at Cessationism's core. As you might imagine, many scholars have attacked Warfield since 1918, but many have agreed with him, too, and have refined his work considerably.[3]

However, the Cessationist view has taken something of a battering from the fact of the dramatic growth of the Pentecostal and charismatic movements which we have already examined. You can't help but lose a bit of credibility if you walk through a forest claiming that there are no longer any such things as trees! We have also become, I suggest, a bit more friendly in the church today towards those who hold differing opinions, and it goes against the grain to claim that wise and respected leaders in different traditions within the church are subject to satanic delusion and heretical error. Postmodernism, as we have mentioned, makes us much more content to say to each other, 'If that's your thing, fine. It's not mine, but if it works for you, go for it!' So the strict Cessationist position lacks a certain popularity which it held even thirty years ago.

But a watered-down version of it has replaced it as the ground has shifted somewhat: the debate tends nowadays to be about 'normality'. OK, we clearly can't say, in the face of the evidence, that there are *no* supernatural manifestations of the Spirit today, and it's not really the ticket to claim that they are all demonic counterfeits, but to what degree is it right to expect them as daily events? If God wants to intervene sovereignly from time to time, who are we to stop him? But that doesn't mean to say that we should ask or expect him to, and it certainly isn't true to say that there is this thing called 'charismatic' which lifts our Christianity on to an altogether different plane.

This view has as its starting point that in the Bible there seem to be distinctive times when the miraculous is much more to the fore. Such 'clusters' of supernatural events can be found around the time of Moses, of Elijah and Elisha, and of course of Jesus and the Apostles. But the rest of the time it all goes rather quiet. We have already noted the ebb and flow of the Spirit's activity throughout church history. Thus, it is concluded, it never was the case that the Spirit was, as it were, 'on tap', but that at some times God chose to crank up the miraculous content of the church's life, while at others he seemed content to let it be. There is also the danger, of course, that an over-concentration on the supernatural gifts of the Spirit can lead to a reduced emphasis on other, less spectacular, bits of real Christian life. People may be more keen to 'get a prophecy' than to settle into the discipline of regular Bible-reading, they may regard the Spirit as in some way 'absent' when he is not doing all his dramatic stuff, and they may underplay the long, slow process of sanctification in which the Spirit is engaged in a quest for the instant and exciting. And in particular, there may be a 'triumphalistic' desire to escape miraculously from the hardships and troubles of real life, rather than recognizing the Spirit's work in producing endurance and joy in suffering. So let's not exclude the possibility of God breaking in supernaturally in some way, but don't let's get hung up on it. If it happens, it happens, but if it doesn't, let's recognize the equally powerful work of the Spirit in other ways.

So how might we evaluate these two similar positions? A good place to begin is always the Bible itself: is there any indication there that the gifts of the Spirit might be only temporary? Warfield claims, of course, that there is, but his biblical work is brief and has been debunked fairly easily by later scholars. However, I want to suggest that there are indeed biblical passages which tell us that the gifts of the Spirit will cease, and it is in precisely those passages that we can find the evidence to dispute Cessationism.

The clearest passage, and the one we will study, since other passages make largely the same point, is 1 Corinthians 13, the famous chapter on love which you've heard read at all those weddings. The key verses are these:

8 Love never fails. But where there are prophecies, they will cease; where there are tongues, they will be stilled; where there is knowledge, it will pass away. *9* For we know in part and we prophesy in part, *10* but when perfection comes, the imperfect disappears. *11* When I was a child, I talked like a child, I thought like a child, I reasoned like a child. When I became an adult, I put childish ways behind me. *12* Now we see but a poor reflection as in a mirror; then we shall see face to face. Now I know in part; then I shall know fully, even as I am fully known.

Quite clearly this passage teaches that the gifts of the Spirit will cease! But the question is, when? Not, as Warfield claims, at the time all the Apostles have popped off, but at the very end of the age. This passage is clearly 'eschatological'; in other words it is looking forward to the time when time will end, Jesus will return and we will be with him for ever. Then, Paul's argument goes, only love will be left, as the temporary manifestations of the Spirit will no longer serve any useful purpose.

The verses in question draw a series of contrasts, which Jon Ruthven helpfully tabulates like this:

vv. 9–10	v. 11	v. 12	v. 12
[Now] we know in part and we prophesy in part	When I was a child I talked like a child I thought like a child I reasoned like a child	Now we see but a poor reflection as in a mirror	Now I know in part
but when perfection comes the imperfect disappears	when I became an adult I put childish ways behind me	then we shall see face to face	then I shall know fully even as I am fully known

In each of the four columns there is a 'before and after' clause. The sense of the passage is that the time for the disappearance of the gifts is to be the time when perfection comes and imperfection disappears, when we are fully mature in Christ, when we see him face to face, and when our knowledge is full. To claim that this time was reached just about the time St John shuffled off his mortal coil is somewhat surprising! It can only possibly refer to the return of Jesus and the end of time, not some arbitrary date around the end of the first century.

This same argument, that the gifts of the Spirit are given to help and strengthen us until the time they are superseded by the return of Christ, is stated or implied in several other New Testament passages, such as 1 Corinthians 1:4–8 and Ephesians 4:7–13. Ruthven in his book discusses these fully, so I needn't bother to do it again here. So in a sense the Cessationists are right: it's just that they've got the date wrong. This biblical evidence, coupled, of course, with the sheer weight of evidence from contemporary Pentecostal/charismatic church growth, makes a full-blown Cessationist position somewhat tricky to maintain today, and few do try to maintain it.

But what of the 'normality' arguments? Is it just Cessationism in retreat, is it nothing more than modified dispensationalism, or are there some real issues to be dealt with? Let's have a look.

Is it wrong to expect the gifts today?

It does indeed seem to be the case that the supernatural comes in clusters in the Bible and throughout church history, but does that of itself mean that to expect supernatural gifts nowadays is erroneous? For a start, might we not be living in such a 'cluster' time? The phenomenal growth of the church world-wide, and the reports of miracles one hears, particularly from the developing world, might indeed be interpreted to suggest that we are experiencing a mighty outpouring of the Spirit, in comparison with which anything in the Bible seems a bit tame. But even if that is not true, and in fact the level of gifting nowadays does not match up to that exhibited in the time of Jesus and the Apostles, does that mean that there are no gifts around at all, or that we shouldn't continue to expect God to work in miraculous ways on a more than occasional basis?

Then, of course, there is the question of exactly what a 'miracle' is. A basic starting definition might be 'something which can only happen if God directly causes it to happen', and we know what that definition is trying to say. Something which is not 'normal' or 'natural' can be called miraculous, but not something which is quite likely to have happened anyway. So if I pray for someone with a migraine and it instantly stops (as has happened to me on a couple of occasions when people have prayed for me) we might call that a miracle, whereas if after prayer the victim went and slept it off and was fine by the morning we might be less inclined to do so. And, of course, the word has changed its meaning in common language: 'It'll be a miracle if United win on Saturday!' speaks of extreme unlikelihood, while 'It's a miracle every time a baby is born!' has more to do with emotional wonder than naturalness. Personally I think it would be a miracle if the baby emerged from its mum's left ear: the natural way is not miraculous, it's perfectly normal! So we come back to the question again: just what is a miracle?

Let's take some extremes. Someone with an amputated leg is prayed for and before everyone's eyes a new leg grows. Now that's what you call a miracle! There is no way that could have happened without the direct intervention of God. But what if the leg was merely broken, and as a result of prayer it healed in about a quarter the time the doctors would have expected. Does that still qualify? Or suppose a Christian is able to speak fluently in a language he hasn't learnt and can't understand? What about that in the miracle stakes? It's not easy, is it? Scholars have argued long and hard about what constitutes a miracle and what doesn't, and all we can say with any degree of certainty is that while there are some things which can only be described as miraculous and others which certainly couldn't, there is a huge grey area in between.

Now, if you apply that to the 'what is normal?' argument, it does change things a bit. It might have been the case that for the Apostles real class-one miracles were daily occurrences (although even that is not certain), but that clearly isn't true of the church in England today. But does that mean that we shouldn't expect even little miracles? If God wants to do a really big one he will (provided the unbelief of the culture around doesn't get in the way and hinder things, as it did when Jesus went back to Nazareth), but I'm still instructed by the Bible to be filled with the Spirit, eagerly to desire spiritual gifts, and so on. If the ebb and flow of the Spirit's power means that I must just sit back and wait *in case* God should decide to do something significant, then I am forced into disobedience to the Bible. But instead I am called, I believe, to live as though the power of God is manifestly present, even when it doesn't seem to be. The Old Testament saints cried out to God in desperation when he appeared to be absent or silent: the cry 'How long, O Lord...' goes up from psalmists and prophets again and again. But now we're told to get on with it and never expect God to do anything dramatic. If he does it'll be nice, but don't hold your breath. Just get on with real life. Somehow I think not!

So I remain unconvinced by any argument which tries to tell me that what has become a normal and valued part of my spirituality is not really happening today. I believe what the Bible says about the supernatural gifts of the Spirit being available *then*, and I see no reason to doubt that they are here for his church *today*. The only tragedy is that much of the church doesn't seem to want them!

Chapter 11

Is 'This' 'That'?

In the chapter about the Bible commanding us to be filled with the Spirit, I flagged up an important question to which I promised to return later. It will be a difficult question to deal with, because it is a very slippery customer indeed. Now is the time to have a go.

As part of my training for the ministry I had to study philosophy, a subject about which I don't think I understood a single word. Many years on I can remember very little about it, and I'm not certain that this has in significant ways damaged my ministry. The one bit I do remember, though, is being asked about a cow in a field. Imagine that you walk through a gate into a field, we were told, and that facing you head on is a cow. Personally I had real problems imagining that, since the cow's presence would have made me stay safely the other side of the gate, not being a great fan of large animals of any description. However, we were on a quest for philosophical truth, so in I went. You decide, my lecturer told us, to walk around the cow. Sidestepping the profound philosophical question 'Why?' I set out to walk around said cow, only to find that as I do so the creature turns on the spot so that at every point she is still facing me head on. But I keep walking and eventually return to my starting point and, with a sigh of relief that I am still alive and ungored, make my exit through the gate. Now, said the lecturer, here comes the philosophical question. Have you or have you not walked round the cow?

Of course I have, I think to myself. Then in that case, ripostes the lecturer, why did you at no point walk past its bottom? Good question. OK, so I haven't walked round it. So what on earth were you doing for five minutes if you weren't standing still? No answer.

This is the stuff, apparently, of philosophy, and provides one reason why Anglican clergy who have studied it are so powerfully and effectively leading their flocks onwards to health, growth and victory. But in spite of my somewhat cynical attitude towards it, the study of philosophy does raise some profound questions, one of which bears on our discussion of the biblical mandate to be filled with the Spirit.

Seeing things

One branch of philosophy, called 'epistemology', deals with questions about how we know things. In particular, how do I know that the way I see something is the same as the way others see the same things?

Show me a tomato, for example, and I will be able fairly confidently to tell you that it is red. I know it's red, and I know that I would also be able to identify a postbox, a ripe strawberry, my friend Janet's car and my favourite Anglican Renewal Ministries eucharistic vestments as being the same kind of red. My wife Chris could be shown the same collection of objects. With a confident flash of insight she also would be able to identify them as red. So we're agreed on that one.

Except that how do I know that what Chris sees as red is the same as I see it? Might she not in fact be seeing what I know to be blue? She might call it red, and she would have grown up in the same world as me where tomatoes and strawberries were known to be red, but it might be the case that what she calls red is what I, if I could see it through her eyes, would instantly recognize as blue.

Of course, the answer to this little dilemma is that for all practical purposes it makes not the slightest bit of difference as long as we are working from the same convention. And no doubt some scientists could find a way of wiring up Janet's car and my tomato and measuring objectively the wavelength of the light reflected from them and assuring us that red really is, after all, red, whoever is looking at it. But questions like this have provided hours of harmless fun for philosophers, and I don't begrudge it to them at all.

How do you know ...?

But the question which we must examine now is much more important, although of the same nature as these two rather silly examples. Let's begin on the day of Pentecost in AD 33 in a street in Jerusalem. You know the story: a group of believers in Jesus who had been praying together in one of the houses suddenly erupted on to the street, having been filled with the Holy Spirit of God, and began to declare the wonders of God in a variety of languages which the cosmopolitan groups of visitors to the city recognized as their own. Peter, one of the believers, stood up to explain what was going on, and in the course of his speech he referred to the Jewish scriptures and the book of the prophet Joel. Joel had prophesied about a coming time when God was going to pour out his Spirit on all his people, so that they would receive prophetic and visionary giftings. In the past, as we have already seen, the Spirit had come upon some people on odd occasions, but Joel's prediction was that the Spirit would come on all people. 'You want to know what's going on now before your very eyes?' said Peter. 'Well, what Joel prophesied is now being fulfilled! "This" which is going on now, is "that" about which Joel spoke.'

See the question coming? 'Peter, how do you *know* that this is that?' And it is exactly this question which many are asking about present-day manifestations associated with charismatic renewal. How exactly do I know that what I see today among charismatics is indeed exactly what the Bible is talking about when it talks about the work of the Spirit? If I overhear a charismatic doing what he calls 'speaking in tongues', how can I be sure that what he is doing is the same thing that Paul and the other New Testament writers were referring to when they wrote about speaking in tongues? Is current charismatic practice really the heir of New Testament Christianity, or might it be some modern monster created by a bunch of loonies living in an over-the-top age?

This is a vitally important question, because up till now I have made some pretty huge assumptions without much evidence to support them. I've looked at the New Testament (the world of which I've obviously never experienced directly: getting old I may be, but not *that* old) and I've looked at the modern charismatic scene (which I do know slightly better), and I've said, 'This is that'. Is it really? A tremendous amount hangs on the answer to this question: if it is the same, the arguments in this book begin to look more and more conclusive, but if it isn't we could be on very dangerous ground indeed, and I could be promoting widespread heresy.

We've gone a little way towards the answer to this question already, of course, in identifying the fact that there is a difference between core charismatic spirituality and the different cultures it gets wrapped up in. Clearly the Bible nowhere instructs me to sing Graham Kendrick songs, play the guitar or wave coloured flags about. Those are just some contemporary accretions about which the Bible is silent and probably neutral – although I do have a sneaking suspicion that God quite enjoys Graham Kendrick, or else why should his stuff get on to *Songs of Praise* so often? The desire to do those things, where it exists, no doubt flows out of some of the values of the core spirituality, but we clearly cannot look at each aspect of contemporary charismatic practice and claim biblical precedent for it, any more than we could with Anglo-Catholicism's candles or Celtic stones and twigs.

But is there any of it for which we can claim biblical precedent? Some would indeed go so far as to say that something as seemingly clearcut as the gift of tongues is open to question. How do we know that a Christian praying in tongues today is doing the same thing as they might have been doing in Corinth? Clearly we cannot, with cast-iron certainty: we can only assume from what we do know of both ends that the bridge does in fact span the years. But it is possible to claim, at least in theory, that like the famous bridge at Avignon, there is a huge gap in the middle.

What about the gift of tongues?

Max Turner discusses this problem with particular respect to the gift of tongues, and some of the evidence he brings does at first sight seem to suggest that there are some differences between the gift as practised then and now. We need to distinguish first of all between what sociologists call 'xenolalia' and 'glossolalia'. Xenolalia, from the same word as xenophobia, means to speak in an unlearnt *foreign* language, while glossolalia describes speech in an unknown and unrecognizable language. So on the day of Pentecost what was going on was clearly xenolalia, since all the worshippers could hear their own native dialects being spoken, such that they were able to understand what was being said or at least that God was being praised. While there are from time to time stories on the charismatic circuit of tongues-speech being understood by foreigners as their own language, most of what goes on is not recognizable. Linguists have researched the gift of tongues long and hard, and the general consensus seems to be that most of it is *linguistic*, as opposed to being gibberish, but that no specific known language is recognizable.[1] But Turner raises several questions about this: how do we know that what was going on, for example in the church in Corinth, was the same as what happened on the day of Pentecost? The view held by some early Pentecostals that the gift of tongues was for witness in foreign missions is not widely believed nowadays, not least because there is no evidence in the New Testament apart from the events of Acts 2 to support it. For Paul, the gift is exclusively for the building up of the individual and church, and never for evangelism (in fact it can work against evangelism – see 1 Corinthians 14:22–3). The Acts 2 use of the gift may be an isolated example of xenolalia, just as isolated examples are to be found today. Paul also allows for the possibility of angelic languages: could this account for them not being recognizable by earthly linguists?

But for Turner the more crucial question has to do with the content rather than the form of tongues. Paul says that the gift should be used for edification, so Turner asks

> whether modern 'tongues-speech' functions in a doxological, christo-centric, faith-supporting (e.g. personality-integrating, cohesive, anxiety-minimising) and upbuilding way? ... The testimony of those who claim the gift – and of a number of the more recent specialist psychiatric investigations – is that it does.[2]

What that means in English is that if Paul says speaking in tongues should glorify God and do you good, and speaking in tongues does indeed do that, it must be OK.

However, in spite of all this clever stuff, I need to come clean and say that I still don't believe we can deal with this question totally conclusively. All we can do is to nibble away at it, to the point where I believe we can go beyond reasonable doubt.

The first thing to say is that the gap between the New Testament and us today is not an empty gap. We have already mentioned the many accounts from virtually every period of church history of people who exhibited the gifting of the Holy Spirit, and there is clearly more continuity than discontinuity. It's not as though everything suddenly stopped without trace a few years after Jesus died and suddenly reappeared from scratch in 1900 (we have already seen that those who would want to claim that the first part of that statement is exactly what did happen are quite simply wrong). There is a high degree of continuity through history, and I am convinced that the onus of proof lies with those who would claim that it is all different nowadays. Charismatics today who read the accounts of some of the things which happened for Augustine, or Anselm, or the Wesleys, would recognize clearly that their own spirituality was in recognizable continuity with that of these saints from the past.

But another way towards an answer would be to ask some questions about how renewal started up again, particularly after periods when it all went relatively quiet. Most people living currently who would claim to have been baptized in the Spirit were no doubt led into that experience by other people. Therefore there is a high degree of probability that they were 'infected' by the culture, theology, presuppositions, and so on, of the person or persons doing the leading. It seems to have been the pattern in the early church that people received the baptism in the Spirit through prayer and laying on of hands by those already experienced, so no doubt there would have been both deliberate catechesis or teaching and unconscious socialization into particular ways of going about things. And, of course, the same has been true of the current charismatic renewal: people have to a high degree been 'taught' what being filled with the Spirit ought to be like. This may not be a bad thing, but it does make the question 'How do we know that this is the real New Testament McCoy?' an important one. To take one very practical example, it is not an uncommon practice in renewal circles, when praying with people to receive the gift of tongues, for the pray-er to pray out loud in tongues herself so that the neophytes can join in and thus get their own language to begin to flow. What that means is that their model is a human one, and there is at least the risk that it might be *merely* a human one. The history of the church is littered with all too many groups and movements who no doubt believed that they were being obedient to the Bible but who went sadly astray, sometimes with disastrous results.

But that isn't true every time. There have been plenty of groups and individuals whose first experience of the Spirit came totally out of the blue, untouched by human hand. Many of the early pioneers of renewal came into the experience by a sovereign act of God. The only guide they had was their reading of the New Testament, and some of them would previously have been negatively disposed towards the view that these manifestations were still around today. Some of the traits of modern charismatic practice may well be learned behaviour read back into the New Testament, but that cannot be true for those whose charismatic experience came directly from God without human intervention, and whose predisposition would have been to disbelieve in a New Testament mandate for these things. And, of course, when they spoke to others of their experience and found that in completely independent ways they too had been led into similar experiences, it served to reinforce their opinion that both their lives and the lives of the others had been impacted by none other than the Holy Spirit of God.

And the other gifts?

Tongues is perhaps a difficult example to study, since it is of such an unusual nature, but other of the Holy Spirit's gifts might not be quite as difficult to deal with. How do we know that 'healing' as ministered today by charismatics is the same as that of the New Testament believers? Presumably because from time to time people get better. Healing is healing, whichever century you're living in. Prophetic gifts, similarly, can be fairly easily seen to be in continuity with the Bible, since we have so much of it there to study and compare with current practice. We can be much more sure about those aspects of renewal than we can about tongues, which by its very nature can only be mentioned in the Bible, and not directly spelt out.

So while we can't prove conclusively that the 'this' of modern renewal is without doubt the 'that' of the New Testament, the evidence, I suggest, is of sufficient strength to suggest beyond reasonable doubt that the core of charismatic spirituality today is in continuity with the Bible. I suspect that those who would argue to the contrary would have every bit as difficult a job on their hands trying to prove to me that there was a definite discontinuity, that 'this' definitely *isn't* 'that'. But I see the evidence as so strong that the onus of proof is on my opponents, not on me. And before I get to sound too much like a barrister, I'd better rest my case!

Chapter 12
....

Word and Spirit

One of the most common arguments used against charismatic renewal is that it claims new revelation from God, and that the Bible clearly teaches that there is to be no new revelation. Talk of charismatic 'prophecies' rings all sorts of warning bells in the kind of evangelicals who place a high value on a belief in the final authority of the scriptures. We have all we need in the written Word, so the argument goes, and any talk of a new thing brought to us by the Spirit is therefore dangerous and probably heretical.

As with most criticisms of just about anything, there is no smoke without fire. There clearly have been those within charismatic renewal who appear to have elevated their own experience to canonical status, and both individuals and groups have gone sadly off the rails because they have done so. Perhaps the most common example is the prediction of the end of the world: Jesus told his disciples that even he didn't know when that would be, but that only the Father knows (Matthew 24:36). The Bible seems to be pretty clear on that point, yet many down the years have thought they knew better, and have, after some kind of supposed 'revelation', predicted specific dates, none of which (so far) has turned out to be accurate. The Bible never emphasizes knowing about when the world will end, but always emphasizes living every day as though it might be the day on which Jesus will return. Such claims to special revelation, which not only go beyond scripture but also contradict its emphases, have quite rightly been treated by the mainstream church as spurious. But that is my point: the mainstream church, and indeed the mainstream of renewal, are agreed that 'prophecies' should not count for more than the written Word of scripture. When someone on the loony fringe disobeys that principle, they are not in any way representing the mainstream. If the gifts of the Spirit, and in particular the revelatory gifts, are seen as being in competition with the Bible, there is no disagreement among any Christians I know: the Bible wins hands down. But is that really how it is? Is it really meant to be the Spirit versus the Bible?

'New' revelation and scripture

When in Chapter 10 we discussed the Cessationist thinking of B.B. Warfield, we noted the false step of logic he made in equating prophetic gifts with 'new revelation'. We will need to explore this important argument, not least because I for one have no desire whatsoever to turn into a heretic ('Too late!' I hear you cry) or to detract from the Bible as the central revelation of God. But before we do so, let's be clear how this argument is being set up: the assumption is that 'new' revelation from God must necessarily contradict scripture: that's why it's so dangerous. But might it be possible to hear afresh from God in ways which don't *contradict* the Bible but which *apply* or *expound* it? Let me illustrate.

It is the custom in the Church of England that when a vicar leaves a church a coach is organized to take people to see him or her inducted to their new job. Although my job with Anglican Renewal Ministries does not entail my running a parish church, I still had to be licensed by the Bishop of Derby, in whose diocese I was to be based, so a coach full of ex-parishioners set off from Coventry to say their last goodbyes and to see me safely installed into my new post.

Derby is not the easiest of cities to drive around, but I had already been working there for a month, and had just about by that stage managed to find the bits of the city I needed. So I had written full instructions for the coach driver, and drawn a very helpful map for him, to get him safely to the church we were borrowing for the evening. I had expected that I would need to arrive early, and so had planned to drive there by car, but in the event there was no need to be early so I joined the coach.

The driver managed to follow my 'M69 – M1 – A52' instructions without too much trouble, but as we approached the city centre I wondered whether he would be grateful for some more specific help, so I got up from my seat and went down to the front and stood beside him, from where I was able to tell him things like 'You want to be in the right-hand lane up here; ignore that slip road there, but begin to edge over so that you can take the next left, which is about 200 yards away; now bear right in front of the Aga Shop and the Flowerpot pub, and keep in the left-hand lane past the Jet garage', and so on. Eventually we found both the church and the bishop, and I was duly licensed.

It seemed to me later, on reflection, that without wanting to give myself ideas above my station, my role on the journey was a little like that of the Holy Spirit to Christians on their journey through life. In particular, the relationship between me and my map is an interesting one for illustrating the relationship between Word and Spirit. The first thing to say is that the map was perfectly adequate for the navigational task in hand. It was drawn by me, and my subsequent revelation did not contradict it or make it unnecessary. But what I did do, in the role of the Spirit, was to apply the written word as each bit became necessary and relevant. I came alongside the driver and said, in effect, 'You know the instructions said turn left? Well, do it *now!*' He could have found the church perfectly well, given enough time, just by using the written instructions, but my presence beside him made his task so much easier, removed any possibility of wrong turns, and got us all there in less of a panic than might otherwise have been the case.

Many people have concerns about the work of the Holy Spirit which are illustrated by this story. 'If we rely on the Spirit,' the rhetoric goes, 'we undervalue the written Word.' In particular, so-called 'prophetic' revelations of the Spirit are viewed with suspicion, since they call into question the once-for-all revelation by God through his written Word which, Christians believe, contains everything we need to know.

Of course, there have been those who have appeared to pay so much attention to 'new' revelation from the Spirit that they have to all intents and purposes ignored the scriptures, but this is not a major fault of all charismatics. In my experience the charismatic renewal most commonly leads people to the Bible, not away from it, and greatly enhances their appreciation of scripture. This is especially true in those parts of the church which have not traditionally paid as much direct attention to the Bible as others: I know of Anglo-Catholic churches which have majored on Bible study groups since they became involved with renewal. The job of the Spirit is not to replace scripture, but to apply it.

Bible deism

Having said that, however, and to be really contentious, there is one exception to this general rule: the story in the Bible of when the Holy Spirit told someone quite directly and specifically to disobey scripture. Acts 10 tells the story of Peter, in a trance on the roof of a house in Joppa, dreaming of a direct command from God to eat animals which his written scriptures expressly forbade him from eating. We are so used to this story that we often fail to see the incredibly radical nature of it: God is bringing new revelation which gives Peter permission to go against all that his background, tradition and steeping in the scriptures have taught him. I often illustrate this by asking pastors what they would do if a young couple from their youth group arrived saying that God had told them in a vision that it was OK for them to move in together. Most of us would point out that to do so would be to disobey the Bible, but the young couple in my scenario would keep on asserting that they knew it wasn't very scriptural but that nevertheless God had told them in this vision that they should do it anyway. That's exactly what happened to Peter, and not surprisingly those above him weren't any keener than modern-day pastors.

Now I am not in any way wanting to build a doctrine for all time on this one biblical passage. Of course, we can see the bigger purposes of God in the grand sweep of the Bible which show this command as being in the eternal plan of the Creator and Redeemer for his people, in a way which is of far more significance than a couple of teenagers shacking up together, but it does make an important point for those who are tempted to elevate the position of the scriptures to too high a place: God himself has the last word. I remember a friend who was due to do a talk about the Bible at an evangelistic course. The notes provided for him listed ways in which the Bible might be good for us: it brings us peace, it brings us guidance – you know the sort of thing. 'I can't tell them that!' my friend exclaimed to me. 'It's Jesus who gives us peace, guidance and all the rest of it, not a book about him!' He had a point. To place the Word of God above God himself is a subtle form of idolatry: like all idolatry it angers God and leads to death, not life.

It is this approach to the Bible, this tendency to exalt it above God himself, which American theologian Jack Deere calls 'Bible deism':

The Deists of the eighteenth century worshipped human reason. The Bible deists of today worship the Bible. Bible deists have great difficulty separating Christ and the Bible. Unconsciously in their minds Christ and the Bible merge into one entity. Christ cannot speak or be known apart from the Bible. At one time Christ did speak apart from the Bible [through dreams, visions, impressions and so on]. However the Bible deist believes that the only one who does these things today is the devil. In fact the devil can do all the things Christ used to do ...

A Bible deist reads passages like Isaiah 28:29:

'All this also comes from the Lord Almighty, wonderful in counsel and magnificent in wisdom ...'

and in his or her mind translates it into something like this:

'All this also comes from the Bible, which is wonderful in counsel and magnificent in wisdom...'

Bible deists read John 10:27 like this: 'My sheep listen to the Bible; I know them, and they follow the Bible.' They hear Jesus say 'If I go away, I will send you a perfect book' (John 16:7).

> Bible deists preach and teach the Bible rather than Christ. They
> do not understand how it is possible to preach the Bible without
> preaching Christ.[1]

Jack Deere's book is well worth studying on this issue of whether or
not we can expect God to speak to us in new ways today. Brought
up as a Bible-believing evangelical, Deere found himself surprised
by the power of the Spirit and by the voice of God in a way which
led him to re-examine his foundations. Like virtually all charismatics, he is profoundly committed to scripture, but he has learnt to
take seriously those parts of scripture which command us to recognize the significance of the supernatural work of the Holy Spirit.
He gradually came to realize that the position he previously held,
and which he would have defended strongly as being a 'biblical'
position, actually came from somewhere much deeper: a desire to
protect the church from the potential errors of subjectivism, and
personal wounds and hurts from the past for which he blamed God
and which therefore made him afraid of God. 'I wanted a personal
relationship with God,' he confesses, 'but I didn't want an intimate
one ... I decided that my primary relationship would be to a book,
not to a Person.'[2]

'By now you've probably figured out that Bible deism is not so
much a theology as it is a system that caters to a personality type,'
he continues. 'It's a system that religiously proud, hurt, intellectual
people find hard to pass up.'[3]

It might just be that a charismatic openness to the Spirit, rather
than devaluing scripture for us, will actually help it to have a more
rightful place in our spirituality, and a place which can bring to our
hurts healing and freedom.

The Spirit and the Bible

So what exactly is the role of the Spirit with respect to the Bible?
Surely it is about applying and interpreting, as was my conversation with the coach driver. The map gives all the information we
need to know, but the divine cartographer is able to say, 'That
bit applies now!' A few years ago I had a profound experience of

reconciliation with a group of people with whom I had previously been at enmity. It happened during a time of worship when the Holy Spirit was deeply at work, and many other people around me were similarly experiencing his power. I knew that I just had to go to someone present, who represented that group, express my penitence, seek their forgiveness and live differently from then on. By God's grace I was, and have been, able to do all these. So what was the role of the Spirit in that encounter? It certainly wasn't to bring new revelation. I had known for most of my Christian life that I was supposed to live in love and peace with all people, rather than holding on to grievances and harbouring animosity and hatred in my heart: the Bible had always told me so. The problem was that however much I wanted to live according to the Bible, I simply hadn't been able to. But now, under the anointing of the Spirit, I had had that area of my life brought into sharp and specific relief, and had received his help to do something about it, something which resulted in a change of heart and of behaviour. Without the work of the Spirit on that occasion I would have been left in my sin and guilt, knowing I was in the wrong but being unable (and indeed unwilling) to do anything about it: with it I became free.

This seems to me to illustrate so much of the Spirit's work, as he applies the written Word in life-changing ways. Perhaps Paul had this kind of thing in mind when he wrote that 'the letter kills, but the Spirit gives life' (2 Corinthians 3:6).

Most Christians would find no trouble in agreeing that we need the Spirit to help us understand and live out the truth of the Bible, and that we need the Bible to check out and test anything which we think might have come from the Spirit. This complementary relationship is surely how it was always meant to work. But to use the very scriptures which urge us to 'desire eagerly the spiritual gifts, especially the gift of prophecy' to argue that we mustn't touch them with a bargepole is surely somehow askew!

Chapter 13

Gifts or Fruit?

Another criticism levelled against renewal spirituality is that we're altogether too obsessed with the gifts of the Spirit, so that we are in danger of forgetting other, less dramatic aspects of his work. In particular, some would say that the *real* work of the Spirit is that of ongoing, unspectacular sanctification, as he slowly and continuously grows in us the 'fruit of the Spirit' which Paul talks about in Galatians 5. How might we begin to address this argument?

The first thing to say is that there is indeed a real danger here, which charismatics ignore at their peril. We live at a time when the search for experience is going on all around us. Charismatics who expect regular encounters with God, who speak commonly of God 'showing up' at meetings and services, and who are often rewarded with exactly what they expect, can fall easily into the trap of thinking that if on one occasion nothing spectacular does appear to happen, God has not shown up and is somehow absent. Sometimes at charismatic meetings when a 'ministry time' is going on, we reward outrageous behaviour by going to pray further for those who are 'manifesting' the Spirit's power in their bodies the most strongly and dramatically, again giving the subtle message that the work of the Spirit is strongest when our physical and vocal reactions to it are strongest. What does that say to those in whom the Spirit is at work in a much more quiet, gentle way, which may simply not be noticeable to others? If we look only for the Spirit at work in the dramatic, we are indeed in danger of missing some of the other equally vital modes of his activity. And if we look only for

121

the work of the Spirit in what is going on now, we may indeed miss his long-term action in our lives and our churches. Many Christians feel, with some justification, that the long-term, almost unnoticeable work of the Spirit is worth far more than the instant and spectacular, but perhaps shallow, things he is doing here and now.

So I don't have a problem with the fruit of the Spirit. It may be that some charismatics seem to talk more about gifts than they do about fruit, and that might be a mistake (although it may not be, as I'll argue in a moment), but I don't know any who would say that the fruit is unimportant, or dangerous, or that it is to be avoided, or that it died out at the end of the apostolic age.

Note, however, once again, how the issue is being set up: 'fruit' is more important, or of more value, or more deserving of our attention, than 'gifts'. And note also how this argument is closely related to the 'What is normal?' one we examined in Chapter 10. We shouldn't expect God to do spectacular things; we should just sit and wait for him to make us holy. We co-operate in that process, of course, but it is this slow, natural, gradual process which is the *real* work of the Spirit.

Once you set up the issue like that, the false step of logic becomes immediately apparent. Two questions are crying out to be asked: is it right to place gifts and fruit in opposition to one another, as though we could only choose to have one or the other, and should we 'seek' the fruit of the Spirit? In each case I'd want to answer with a resounding 'No!'

Seeking the fruit?

Let's take them in reverse order: should we seek the fruit? There are several passages in the New Testament which exhort us to some pretty hard work when it comes to sanctification. We are to resist, flee from, abstain from all that is evil, and cultivate instead good habits of behaviour. We've already looked at the Ephesians passage which says this, and there are plenty more which say more or less the same thing. This is meant to be hard work! The Hebrew Christians got a telling off because they had not yet got to the point of having their blood shed in their struggle against sin (Hebrews 12:4).

But the passage which deals with the fruit of the Spirit, Galatians 5:16–26, is very different in nature. Paul begins with a list of some of the acts which come out of the sinful nature, and a nasty list it is too. From idolatry to immorality to rage and witchcraft, they are all things which we are likely to do if the sinful nature controls us. But then, by way of contrast, Paul lists some of the things which result from the Spirit's influence; love, joy, peace and the rest. Can you spot the difference? The first, nasty list is a list of *acts*, but the second set are *characteristics*. You can *do* witchcraft, but you can *be* gentle. This fruit of the Spirit is not so much about how we behave, but rather about who we are.

But there is a second difference which is even more important. Let's compare the Galatians passage once again with Ephesians 4–5. Look what the author tells those Ephesians to do: to *put off* their old way of life and their falsehood, to *stop* stealing, to *prevent* unwholesome talk coming from their mouths, to *get rid of* bitterness and the rest, to *exclude* sexual immorality and impurity, and to *avoid* the fruitless deeds of darkness. Sounds like hard work, doesn't it? But now look at what the Galatians passage tells them to do: they are to live by the Spirit, and to keep in step with the Spirit. See the difference? In order to avoid evil deeds we have to work hard at excluding them, but to develop good qualities or characteristics, all we have to do is to let the Spirit in. Nowhere are we told to 'seek' the fruit of the Spirit, to work at it, or even to 'desire' it. We are simply to keep in step with the Spirit.

Fruit versus gifts?

In dealing with the second of our two questions we have actually answered the first as well. It is surely not biblical to place fruit and gifts in some kind of opposition to one another and to ask, in effect, for Christians to choose which one they are going to focus on, or which they want in their lives. The two go hand in hand, and you can't really have one without the other.

It might not be by accident that Paul refers to these positive character traits as 'fruit'. Consider an apple tree. Maybe you can even picture one you know well. Have you ever seen it *trying* to have apples? Standing there straining and grunting and pushing until suddenly – pop! an apple appears! None of mine has ever done that. None of mine has actually ever produced any apples at all as far as I can remember, but we'll tiptoe past that one since it rather shoots my clever argument in the foot. The point about fruit is that at least in theory it just grows. The tree gets its roots deep into the ground, all the nutrients flow through its sap, and slowly and gradually, over a period of time, the fruit begins to form, becomes visible, and ripens to full maturity. Cut off that flow of sap and the fruit wouldn't grow properly, but let it flow and the fruit will appear. That's the way trees work (in theory).

And, of course, unless it is a highly intelligent tree, it probably wouldn't even have noticed that it was getting fruit. That's another characteristic of the fruit of the Spirit: you don't notice that it is growing in you: others do. Have you ever had the humbling experience of someone telling you how great you are as a Christian, how helpful your advice was, how caring you were to them in a time of trouble, or whatever? Did you feel genuinely surprised, and totally unworthy of their praise? That's the fruit of the Spirit. Others can see it as clearly as daylight in us, and we can see it in them, but ourselves? Never! In fact the more you ponder your own growth in Christ, the more you feel you haven't even left the starting blocks yet. The fact is, the more holy you become, the more unholy you feel. That's because as you get closer to God you can begin to see yourself as he sees you, and judge yourself by his standards rather than by your own. We've all met brand new Christians who are cock-a-hoop because since they met Jesus three weeks ago they've managed to give up swearing or some other highly offensive sin. They've really arrived, and are so proud of their sanctification. But then you meet an old saint who has been walking with Christ for decades, and whom you consider is about to start sprouting angel's wings, and all they can say is how unholy they feel because they only prayed for four hours yesterday and the Lord has shown them how desperately proud they are in their heart, and so on. The more holy you get, the more you realize how unholy you are: that's the paradox of discipleship.

An obsession with the fruit of the Spirit, therefore, is a highly unhealthy thing. If we're constantly looking in the mirror to see how loving, joyful, peaceful and all the rest we've become, we've missed the point. It's not for us to see, and even if we could see, we'd feel more depressed, not more pleased with ourselves.

So fruit is not for seeking. But the gifts of the Spirit? That's a different matter. As we've seen, we're to seek them earnestly. Surely that answers our first question. Is it a case of making a choice about whether we're going to go for gifts or fruit? No more than a tree chooses between sap or fruit. The picture Paul uses seems clearly to suggest that it is precisely by opening ourselves to the Spirit, by living in his power, and by keeping in step with all he wants to do with us, that his fruit will grow in us. We don't grow the fruit in our lives by self-conscious trying, but simply by allowing the power of the Spirit free flow in our lives. In the same way, if we do open up to the Spirit, we can't help but grow the fruit, whether we like it or not, and even whether we notice it or not. But to cut ourselves off from his power and life and to seek the fruit as an end in itself seems to me to be nonsense, and pretty dangerous nonsense at that, since we will have cut ourselves off from the very thing which is designed to make the fruit grow.

What this means is that those who are most open to the power and goodness of the Spirit ought to be those most exhibiting his fruit, and conversely that those who are opposed to the things of the Spirit run the risk of being unloving, joyless, anxious, impatient, and so on. Far be it from me to suggest that this is always true in real life, but it certainly can be. There can be a hard-edgedness in some Christians which is all about defending strongly held doctrinal convictions but which can very quickly turn ugly. In my work with Anglican Renewal Ministries I get to speak to all sorts of different people from all sorts of different sections of the church: Anglo-Catholics, Liberals, Charismatics, you name it. I get all sorts of reactions when I speak, as you might imagine, but there is one thing I am very sad to report. I report it not out of animosity, but simply because I have observed it to be true: if I am going to get attacked viciously in the question time or during the coffee break, it will invariably be when I am speaking to a group with the word 'evangelical' in their title. No other brands of Christians have ever dished out to me the sort of invective I can get from conservative evangelicals, however deeply they may have disagreed with what I said. It doesn't happen every time I speak to evangelicals, of course: the vast majority are as gracious and gentle as anyone else. But sometimes their zeal for biblical truth and sound doctrine, along with a deeply held position of closedness to what charismatics would see as the renewing work of the Holy Spirit, can make them act towards someone who threatens their views or appears to be trying to teach false doctrine, in ways which I can only describe as vicious. On the other hand I have seen people who, when they have opened themselves to the power of the Spirit, have had their hard edges rubbed off and become much more gentle and good to be with, much more patient with those with whom they disagree, and much more quick to listen than to criticize. Let me say again, it is not that all charismatics are nice and all non-charismatics are nasty; clearly that's nonsense. But to open ourselves fully to the gifting and empowering of the Spirit can be good for us, and can be the source of the Spirit's life which in time will grow in us his character-building fruit.

I'm sure charismatics do have much to learn about seeing God at work in the long-term, unspectacular work of the Holy Spirit, and recognizing that to be real it doesn't have to be noisy. I'm sure that the way they talk and act can sometimes seem to suggest that they value gifts more than fruit. But since the two simply cannot be separated, and since the Bible tells us eagerly to desire the gifts presumably because that will result in us getting fruit too, I wouldn't say that they were committing major heresies worth worrying about too much!

Chapter 14

Promises, Promises

We must now examine another frequent criticism of renewal, that it makes promises which it cannot keep and is fundamentally dishonest in the claims it makes, for example, of miraculous healing. Many critics, particularly of John Wimber, have attacked renewal on these grounds, and we will need to take their questions seriously since, if true, they really do constitute a serious blow against all that I have been arguing for so far.

Let me try to break down this problem into bite-sized bits, so that we know what exactly we're trying to deal with here. It seems to me that several issues are bound up together in this one big question, which, for convenience, we might articulate as 'Does charismatic renewal really work?'

Let's note, first of all, that this criticism is usually based on the 'normality' question which we looked at in Chapter 10. Most of these critics would want to affirm that God might well heal, but that the sheer amount of healings claimed by charismatics must make many of them spurious. This is fundamentally a *theological* issue, and I don't need to go into it again here since I've already said my piece on it, although I will return to it at the end of this section from a different angle.

Second, there is a *pastoral* issue, as critics usually have a stock of stories about people who have been severely damaged, or at the very least disappointed, usually because a longed-for healing had not taken place, or a degree of healing was experienced but did not last.

Third, there is a *ministry* issue to do with the extravagant claims of some charismatic 'healers' who promise healing and then move into denial if it simply doesn't happen for their victims.

And fourth, there is a large question of *integrity* about claims for healing which are not proven to the satisfaction of the critics.

Underlying all these, of course, is an issue of *semantics*: what exactly is a healing, or a miracle? 'When I use a word,' said Humpty Dumpty to Alice in Lewis Carroll's *Through the Looking-Glass*, 'it means just what I choose it to mean.' Charismatics have often been accused of playing the same game with the miraculous, and some critics want a far more objective definition of terms than charismatics have previously bothered with.

So there are some of the issues: can we begin to answer those critics who claim that renewal is all big-mouth-and-trousers with no proof at all of its reality?

The ministry issue

Let me deal quite easily with the ministry issue. Yes, there have been those who have set themselves up as 'healers', who have looked at times as though they, and not Jesus, were meant to be the centre of attention. They have often been flamboyant and extravagant, and they have at times promised healings which they have been unable to deliver. Their behaviour has been manipulative, and may even at times have become downright abusive. There is no way I could deny these accusations, and all I can do is to say that I am deeply sorry for the hurt and distress such figures may have caused. I am particularly distressed that some of them have fallen from grace and been publicly exposed in sin or at least shadiness, dragging the reputation of a whole movement down with them. In slight defence I would say that this matter of ministry *style* is one of the remaining distinctions between charismatic renewal and Pentecostalism (with a capital 'P'), and that I do not generally see such flamboyance among charismatics, who by and large are more careful and restrained than their Pentecostal brothers and sisters. Most charismatics have been influenced in their style of prayer ministry not by Pentecostals but by John Wimber, who would frequently denounce the 'posturing' of other styles of ministry. John was particularly well received by Anglicans, who can usually sniff out humbug at 300 paces, because his style resonated with their values of gentle politeness and dignity. But that is not to excuse the behaviour of some 'healers': as a representative of renewal I can only apologize for it.

But is it really as easy as that? What of the personal cost to those who have believed they were promised healing, only to find that it just didn't happen for them? One of the most frequent stories I hear from clergy, told in many different guises but always with a deeply concerned tone of voice, is of 'a lady from my congregation' who went to such-and-such a meeting, received prayer for healing, and had nothing whatsoever happen. The story continues with the pastor's caring ministrations to the devastated victim, usually referred to as 'picking up the pieces', after which he or she finally manages (or in some variations of the tale doesn't manage) to prevent complete loss of faith, if not nervous breakdown or suicide.

I do, however, have a bit of a problem with such heart-rending stories. It's not that I don't believe they actually happened; I have no doubt of that at all. It's just that they have never happened to me. In fact, they only ever seem to happen to conservative evangelicals. Now doesn't that strike you as a bit strange? I have spent sixteen years in parish ministry, and for at least fourteen of those years I have been in churches where prayer for healing was regularly on the agenda, weekly at Sunday services as well as at different times during the week. During that time I must have seen literally hundreds of unanswered prayers and disappointed victims, but *never once* has anyone come to me saying they were losing their faith as a result. If anyone was devastating people in their church, it surely ought to have been me! I'm really good at getting my prayers not answered: I could do it for England. So where are all the casualties from *my* churches? Neither, lest you are thinking that I'd be the last person my own flock would confide in, have I ever had to deal with such crises from other people's churches.

In fact, most people I have had as parishioners have learnt to accept the fact that healing doesn't always work, but have felt willing to give it a go anyway. They never once heard me invite them down to the front because 'God is going to heal you'; but they often heard me invite them down to the front 'because God wants to minister to you'. Very few would say that in each prayer-encounter they received nothing whatsoever from God, even though very few would say they received complete and instantaneous healing. But they kept coming back for more, and no-one seemed to be that bothered, certainly not to the point of needing their pieces picking up or losing their faith.

All this makes me ask, you see, where these agonized pastoral crises are coming from. They don't seem to be a major characteristic of charismatic churches which do fundamentally believe in healing, but rather of those conservative churches which don't, or at least only in carefully measured doses about once every ten years. I'm sorry, but I can't help but wonder if somehow the pastor, or the church culture, is subtly creating the crisis, in order to back up deeply rooted prejudices.

Take a very practical example. The ubiquitous 'lady from my congregation' goes to such-and-such a meeting and receives prayer for healing, after which nothing whatsoever happens. She reports back to me as her pastor. With my fundamental belief that we ought to expect God to heal, and my support of said meeting as basically a good thing, I listen to her disappointment, empathize with her, explain again that healing is not always instantaneous and that sometimes we have to go on seeking God, and ask if she'd like me to pray for her a bit more now. She goes on her merry way reassured and determined to keep looking to God, whether or not he comes up with her particular set of goods.

But imagine if I'd handled that pastoral encounter in a different way, coming out of my basic disbelief in healing as something to expect, and my slight annoyance that she should have gone off somewhere to another, somewhat suspect, meeting instead of coming to hear me expounding the Word back at home. Nevertheless I muster all my pastoral skills, and nod my head gravely as she recounts her sorry tale. 'That must have been totally devastating for you!' I say, after a polite while. I then go on to explain the evils of charismatic healers, the damage they can do to vulnerable people, and the need for her to get herself rooted back into scripture, which of course nowhere teaches that Jesus might ever heal people. Her faith is saved by my gallant pastoral ministrations, and equilibrium is restored to another wobbly Christian life as the evil errors of the charismatics are resisted.

Now obviously I'm caricaturing, but can you see the point? It just is not within my experience that people have been damaged by sensitive and Spirit-led charismatic prayer ministry. I'd love to have even one story of my own to tell you, but I simply haven't. So whose crisis is it anyway? And where is the balanced and biblical teaching in the church which puts healing in its place, neither promising it as a divine right nor restricting it to a special act of God but don't hold your breath?

Looking for proof

But does it really ever work, or in such quantities that it's worth bothering about? This is the line taken by some critics, often with a medical background, who, conditioned by their scientific training, want Proof. The problem is that here we face a clash of cultures. Charismatics simply don't seem to be interested in proof. They know what has happened to them, and that is enough. They simply refuse to play the proof game. They are not out to prove anything to anyone, and they are not interested in taking their experiences to the scientists for their scrutiny. This is not simply due to fear of their claims proving to be unfounded, as some suggest. It is just that they can't be bothered. They know that something real has happened, and that is enough for them. Why should they have to convince anyone else? This attitude frustrates the proof-merchants tremendously, of course, but that is just too bad.

David Lewis is a social anthropologist who is fascinated by claims for healing. He comes from a position which is basically positive towards renewal and healing, but is determined to apply his science rigorously to the claims of charismatics. In 1985 he attended John Wimber's 'Signs and Wonders' conference in Sheffield, and his brief report on the event was published as an appendix to John's *Power Healing*.[1] This report generated sufficient interest to gain Lewis an invitation to conduct an in-depth study of

Wimber's conference the following year in Harrogate. Here, 2,470 questionnaires were handed out to the conference delegates; 1,890 were returned, and 100 people, chosen at random, were followed up with in-depth interviews between 6 and 12 months later. Lewis then examined both the statistical evidence and some of the personal stories.

He notes, as I have above, the extreme difficulty of defining 'healing' and of gathering objective information. For most minor ailments a doctor would have only the patient's description of the symptoms, and treatment or a prescription would be issued on the patient's subjective description of the problem.

> In many cases all the doctor would be able to say [after an alleged divine healing] is that the patient has ceased requesting repeat prescriptions for a drug or that the patient no longer reports having various symptoms. It is the patient's own account which is the primary evidence of the person's state of health.[2]

Lewis quotes from a personal letter from David Wilson, Dean of Postgraduate Medical Education at Leeds University, which comments on the first draft of his book:

> As a doctor I am troubled by the way in which you give 100 per cent credence to the 'doctor's diagnosis' ... I am so conscious that (a) doctors are not always right, (b) they are very reluctant to admit that anything other than the treatment they prescribed can have benefited the patient ... You are just reflecting the lay public's blind faith in the medical profession.[3]

Some 'healings', of course, can be medically authenticated, at least beyond the reasonable doubt of an objective observer with no theological axe to grind. 'At least some healings following prayer are inexplicable within the frame of reference of conventional medicine. Following Rex Gardner, we may use the adjective "miraculous" to describe such cases.'[4]

But many cannot be so authenticated, and the description of them as miracles is risky, to say the least. Let me tell you a personal story: after a cold a few years ago I had a small lump come up on the inside of one eyelid. Like most people I avoid doctors if I can, so I left it for a few weeks, but when there was no sign of it going away I finally gave in and had it diagnosed as a meibomian cyst, which is like a stye but on the inside of the eyelid rather than the outside. It could be very simply removed at the local eye hospital by a small snip under local anaesthetic, I was told, so an appointment was duly made. But as the day grew nearer I got more and more scared. It wasn't the snip which bothered me: it was the thought of having a needle in my eye for the anaesthetic. On the day of the op the staff team at my church prayed for me, for courage more than for healing. When I went to the hospital the doctor was unable to find anything at all to snip, so I was sent home, to my great relief. So was that a miracle or not? Meibomian cysts do apparently clear up of their own accord sometimes: it might have started getting better weeks earlier, but I just hadn't noticed. It was medically verified in that one doctor had diagnosed it and another had been unable to find it, but that of itself doesn't prove divine intervention. And, as you might imagine, the last thing on my mind was to have anyone else poking around for a second opinion: I had avoided an operation and I was happy to give thanks to God and forget the whole scary incident!

So proof of healing is not easy to get hold of. But even given this kind of difficulty, can we say that anything miraculous actually took place at Harrogate? Lewis' initial answer to that is both positive and negative: 'Among the 1,890 questionnaires from the Harrogate conference there are only 86 cases of total healing claimed for physical conditions.'[5]

According to the questionnaires, 621 people claimed that they had received prayer for physical healing. Of these, 42 per cent said that the prayer had had little or no effect, 26 per cent claimed some degree of healing, and the remaining 32 per cent experienced significant or total healing. This figure seems low, particularly at a conference which was centred around healing, although the good news is that some healing, to some degree, clearly did occur. In examining some individual case-studies, Lewis uncovers some examples which were medically verified, as well as cases where healing was followed later on by recurrence of the condition. At the end of the day Lewis' work is inconclusive: it neither rules out the possibility of miraculous healing nor proves that it happened in vast quantities. What was true of the particular conference in question is no doubt true of the charismatic healing ministry generally: God does heal, but perhaps not as often as we would like, and not as often as is sometimes claimed. Nevertheless, it does seem appropriate to continue to seek God for healing, since it does occur at least sometimes.

But that of itself may not be totally good news, and can raise other issues. An over-emphasis on 'Signs and Wonders' can damage the church, contends Geoffrey Lay:

> John Wimber has been, in large part, responsible for the growth of a Christian mentality which says that a healthy church is one in which miracles are regularly seen. My reasonable and moderate contention is that they are rare.[6]

So we're back to the normality argument again. But there is a more sinister side to this question. Lay, an Anglican priest currently working in Ely diocese, is blind. He and his wife lost their daughter, born disabled, after five agonizing months of watching her little body in almost constant spasm. And on top of all that, they have had to contend with enthusiastic charismatics who wanted to see healing. The 'Signs and Wonders' mentality, Lay claims, has not only fed the church a lie about the expected regularity of healing, but has robbed the church of a proper and caring response to disability. He goes down the route of distinguishing 'curing' from 'healing', stating that

> Cure is only one aspect of wholeness, of health, of salvation. The narrowness of 'signs and wonders' theology lies precisely in the poverty of its understanding of *soteria* (salvation) as *iomai* (cure) which it seeks in the form of miracle.[7]

He continues:

> Salvation is our complete healing and cure is only partial. What is
> most important about Jesus is that he saves. It is also important,
> though considerably less so, that he cures. It is not necessary for me
> to be cured in this life in order for me to be saved.[8]

I agree entirely, but I do find it difficult to go along with those who
take this argument to what I consider to be its illogical conclusion:
the use of the term 'whole' to describe someone not 'cured' but
'saved', and the devaluing almost to the point of non-existence of
the significant healing ministry of Jesus as if it were in some way a
kind of addendum to his preaching, which was what he *really* came
to earth to do.

So can we move onward from this stalemate? Most of us would
agree, I think, with two facts: that truly miraculous healing does
occur, and that it doesn't occur as often as some of us would like it
to, or as often as some of us think the New Testament suggests
it should. What's the problem, and does it invalidate all manifestations of charismatic spirituality?

First of all, it has to be said that this problem is predominantly
a Western middle-class dilemma. The preoccupation with 'proof' is
a manifestation of a modernist mindset which wants to exalt science above faith and set it as judge and jury over the subjective
claims of Christians. It really is important to us to prove all sorts of
things, lest someone might have got something wrong, which
would never, never do. The complete absence of this fascination
with empirical proof in the developing countries may be one
contributing factor for the much higher incidence of miraculous
healing which one hears reported from those who have ministered
overseas. People whom we in the West might patronizingly describe
as somewhat 'primitive' and 'naïve' seem to have so much less of a
problem with taking the New Testament at face value and believing
it. Our whole culture, built as it is on Cartesian doubt (the basic
assumption that things are guilty until proven innocent, or unreal
until proved real) must surely create in the church an atmosphere
more of doubt than of faith, an atmosphere which easily crosses the
line into cynicism. This type of general background prevented even
Jesus from performing any miracles when he returned to his home

town of Nazareth (Mark 6:1–6). 'Isn't this the carpenter? Isn't this Mary's son and the brother of James, Joseph, Judas and Simon? Aren't his sisters here with us?' asked the crowd, thinking no doubt that they knew Jesus and had got him well and truly sewn up. 'He does wardrobes and coffee tables, not miracles!' They took offence at him, but in the process limited his power. This attitude seems to me characteristic of a Western church which thinks it understands Jesus and in the process tames him. And anyway, it may be a hard fact that miracles only occur rarely, but does that necessarily mean that it is meant to be like that?

Personally, I owe a tremendous debt to John Wimber for reminding the church in this country that it perhaps needn't be, even if he did overstate his case at times. Actually I think that people like Geoffrey Lay often overstate theirs in seeking to do down the ministry of John Wimber. He may indeed have had his theological weaknesses – for example, his undeveloped theology of the 'natural' with its tendency to see absolutely everything in terms of either angels or demons but rarely ever viruses. But the juxtaposition of his ministry alongside that of Morris Cerullo in Lay's book, or the implication that he believed all sicknesses to be *directly* demonic in nature[9] are at the very least careless.

The 'dissatisfaction' of the Spirit

So what are charismatics to do? Their reading of the Bible and their experience of the Spirit will not allow them to sink into a fatalistic 'hope-for-the-best' approach to the miraculous, but real life certainly does fall short of what they hope it might be like, at least in England. The answer, I believe, lies in the very nature of the work of the Holy Spirit himself. I owe this insight to a stunning seminar led at New Wine 1999 by Anglican charismatic theologian Graham Cray, material which as far as I am aware has not been written up anywhere so I'll have to do my best for you with some edited highlights. The seminar was entitled 'The Spiritual Gift of Dissatisfaction'.

Most of us are dissatisfied most of the time, but for the wrong reason. As consumerists in a consumerist culture we are constantly living with a broken promise. Consumerism promises to deliver the goods of personal satisfaction and fulfilment, but we soon discover that the buzz comes not from owning stuff, but from the act of buying it. So we become addicted to shopping, and litter our lives with things we've bought in the hope they'd make us feel better but which simply don't for more than a day or two. In other words, we're dissatisfied because of the past: what we hoped for hasn't happened.

It is the job of the Holy Spirit to make us dissatisfied not about the past but about the future. We have already seen his role as the one who equips us for mission and ministry, who thrusts us out into the world to engage with it and its victims in gloriously liberating evangelism. But there is another side to his work, what the New Testament describes as 'firstfruits' or 'deposit'. In Jewish culture there were two, not just one, Harvest Festivals, a thought to strike terror into the hearts of most Anglican clergy! The full knees-up when all was safely gathered in was preceded seven weeks earlier by the festival of 'Firstfruits', when the very first bits of the crops were gathered and offered to God (if you're interested you can read about this in Leviticus 23). The first offering was an act of faith that in due time God would give the full harvest, a celebration of his goodness before there was any evidence to demonstrate it. The Holy Spirit, says Paul in Romans 8:23, is the firstfruits of our redemption. God has given us his Holy Spirit as a promise of all that he intends to give us in the future.

The idea of a 'deposit' is similar. This language is used in 2 Corinthians 1:22 and 5:5 and Ephesians 1:14 to describe God's gift of the Holy Spirit as a down-payment for the full amount to be handed over in the future. When I book a holiday I pay the travel agent a deposit first, to commit myself to using them and to prove that I am serious about my booking. Nearer the time I pay the full amount which my deposit guaranteed.

But what effect do these firstfruits and down-payments have? They draw us towards the future. My travel agent sits there day after day rubbing his hands with glee at the thought of all that money which will come his way when I finally pay up. The few odd sheaves of early grain raise the eyes of the community to the riches of the full harvest. My onion bhaji only serves to make me more hungry for the Lamb Sri Lanka with mushroom pulao rice and keema naan which is to follow. (Not strictly a biblical illustration, that one, but I think you'll agree that it reinforces the point nicely.) So what is the role of the Spirit understood as firstfruits? Surely to make us even more certain of and eager for our full redemption.

And there's the rub. You see, the Spirit has two jobs which keep us looking in two directions at once, rather like the crowd at Wimbledon. He earths us in the real world and calls us to live in it and minister to it now, but at the same time he lifts our sight to heaven and the future. One writer describes that experience in terms of being stretched on the rack as in mediaeval torture chambers. Our feet are tied at one end, and our hands at the other, and we are left in the agonizing position of being strung out between the two. The more the wheels at each end are turned, the more it hurts.

Staying on the rack

So what do we try to do? If we possibly can, we try to untie ourselves from one end or the other. It doesn't really matter which; either will do the trick and release the tension. And that is exactly what Christians have been doing down the years. Some have untied their feet, disengaged from the world and its pain, and lived in the glorious hope of heaven, watching and waiting for their rescue to come from the skies in the shape of the end of the world, revival, some new phase of blessing, or whatever else God may choose to do. 'Heaven is in my heart' is their theme tune, and life goes on in uninterrupted glory. You want healings? They've got them, by the cartload, because that's what heaven is like: no more tears, mourning, crying or any of that stuff. And if it doesn't work, we just pray harder, and sooner or later it's bound to happen!

But others, eschewing this other-worldly triumphalism, untie their hands instead. Their feet are firmly on the ground, walking with the poor and broken through the open sewers of life, empathizing deeply and doing what little they can here and there to make this world a slightly better place. Heaven is for the future, but don't wait for it: there's hard work to do down here, and it's up to us to do it. It's no use sitting waiting for some interventionist God to step in and start fiddling around with the natural order: he's given us the nous to do that for ourselves.

You see, in one or other of these two ways most Christians have untied themselves from the rack, simply to avoid the pain and make themselves feel better. The problem is that in doing so they have escaped from and negated one side or the other of the Spirit's work in their lives. The work of the Spirit is precisely to keep us on the rack, with both ends firmly attached. That's where the agonized groaning of Romans 8:22–4 comes from. We share in the frustration and the bondage to death and decay of all the creation of which we are a part, yet we groan with hope because of the redemption which we know is coming. And we can be sure it's coming, because the very Spirit who inspires the groans is the promise of the inheritance which is ours in Christ. It's a desperately uncomfortable place to be, but at the end of the day it is where we're meant to be. It doesn't much matter whether we escape into charismatic triumphalism, dry evangelical textualism or the liberal death-wish: any of them get us off the rack and therefore out of God's will equally effectively. To escape dissatisfaction in order to make ourselves feel better is to lose the plot.

For me this issue manifests itself most strongly in the area of healing. My Bible holds out for me a vision of the church as a healing community where lost and broken people can find salvation and wholeness, including the 'curing' of their bodies, but my church tells a different story. I could escape either way, should I choose to do so, either with falsified claims of doubtful miracles to pretend something has happened, or with semantic games to explain why I never expected anything to happen in the first place. But I have chosen to stay agonized on the rack, because that's where I believe I should be. I can't with integrity claim in this chapter that charismatic healing always works, or that there aren't from time to time bad practices and spurious claims. Of course I can't. But neither can I give in to the miserable spirituality of the 'it-might-happen-but-it-isn't-meant-to-be-normal' brigade. We're called, I believe, to live in that place of stretching, with our feet firmly planted in the real world of pain and suffering as we work for the gospel and make the best sense we can of the apparent reluctance of God to do anything, while keeping our hands raised heavenwards in hope and prayer for that miraculous inbreaking of divine power.

And in this task there is one further word of comfort and encouragement from Graham Cray's seminar. This is indeed about the inbreaking of divine power. We tend in our culture to base our expectations of the future on our experience of the past. We think in terms of 'progress' or 'progression', and not on what God might sovereignly decide to do *now*. Graham points out that these ideas of progress are Darwinian and ultimately worldly. Rather, in the economy of God, the Spirit teaches the Bride to say, 'Come'. Spirit-inspired prayer is indeed prayer for an inbreaking, and in that light we can see unlimited hope for the future. The more we can glimpse, through the Spirit, of what God might intend for his church and for the world he so loves, the more our hearts expand to contain it, like a balloon being filled from a water tap. We can change! Things might get better! We don't have to base what will be on what has been! That surely ought to be good news!

I began this chapter by formulating the central question as 'Does charismatic renewal really work?' I believe that fundamentally it does, not because it always delivers miracles on tap, but because if it is thoughtful and educated it helps keep us on that stretching-rack, right in the centre of the Spirit's will for us. The church in England is just emerging from the long dark tunnel of modernist anti-supernaturalism, but might just get dazzled by the bright lights of pentecostal fervour. It seems to me vital that we stay where we should be, stretched between heaven and earth, present reality and future hope, and I believe a mature charismatic spirituality will help to keep us there.

Chapter 15

The Death of a Movement?

The final objection which I want to discuss is perhaps the most serious one that has been levelled against charismatic renewal. Paradoxically it comes not from liberals or conservative evangelicals, the two groups which have traditionally shown the strongest opposition to renewal, but from within the charismatic scene itself. The gist of this argument is that charismatic renewal was indeed a gift from God to his church to help us rediscover the Spirit's power, but that somewhere along the line charismatics lost the plot and went off the rails into heresy.

A variation on this theme which does come from the conservative evangelical world is that renewal was always apostate from the very start, but since the gist of these two criticisms is pretty much the same I'll tackle them together. The reason for this diversion from the truth is similar according to all the critics: charismatics were always, or at some point became, obsessed with experience or with the latest renewal fad, and in the process forgot scripture. The particular point at which they did so varies according to different critics, but the end result is the same: charismatics do not hold an evangelical view of, respect for or obedience to the Bible.

Recent trends in renewal

It is indeed a historical fact that renewal over the past thirty years or so has moved through different phases, as new sub-movements have arisen or new gurus emerged. In my short lifetime we have seen the rise of the New Churches, the ministry of John Wimber, the 'Prosperity Gospel' of Kenneth Hagin and co., the Kansas City prophets, deliverance ministry in the style of Bill Subritsky and Ellel Grange, the 'Nine O'Clock Service' in Sheffield, 'Revival' at Pensacola, Alpha, the Toronto Blessing, the healing missions of Morris Cerullo, the quest for British revival, and latterly manifestations of gold dust and dental fillings, and people hovering ten feet up in the air as they worship. Quite a bewildering variety, you'll agree.

Some of these movements, characters or events, of course, are relatively easy to deal with. I'm not aware of any in the mainstream of British renewal who look with total favour on the 'Prosperity Gospel' movement, for example. This is based on a few verses from the Old Testament which seem to promise that Christians should know complete health, wealth and happiness as a result of following Jesus. Whatever its proponents may actually be saying, what is most commonly heard is that the movement promises financial wealth, and some of the more extreme examples have promised financial wealth to those who give generously to the particular 'ministry' in question. Critics note with interest that this particular manifestation of church is exclusively a Western phenomenon, and appeals not to the poor of the developing world, who ought surely to need it most, but to relatively rich Western capitalists. They also note, more significantly, that Jesus in the gospels seems to promise exactly the opposite to his followers, commanding them to get rid of accrued wealth rather than to collect even more, in order that they can travel light in their journey with the gospel. My personal take on it is that proponents of this message have confused individual prosperity with community prosperity. I have no problem believing that a town or city which espouses Christian values can become more prosperous (I'll go into the transformation of communities further in Chapter 18). But I'm not at all convinced that the Bible teaches that as an individual Christian I have a divine right to expect that my bank balance will grow. And if God does choose to bless me financially, it is surely only because he wants that money to be available for his wider work, and not because he wants me to replace my Mondeo with a Merc. There is no way in which mainstream British charismatic renewal has embraced the prosperity movement: it is simply unfair to condemn all charismatic renewal along with it.

The story of the Nine O'Clock Service is slightly more complex, but there is still not vast disagreement over it. I had the privilege of being on the staff of St Thomas' Church in Crookes, Sheffield, during the time of the birth of NOS, and I was personally involved with it until I moved to Coventry in 1989. The general consensus is that it was a God-given idea which went horribly wrong due to human weakness and sin. It ought to serve as a warning to the rest of the church, but of itself it does not provide sufficient grounds for writing off renewal as a whole.[1]

Similarly, the ministry of Morris Cerullo with its suspect claims to healing miracles and alleged manipulative behaviour does not really represent mainstream renewal, and many Christians, including the Evangelical Alliance, have raised questions about his methodology and style.[2]

But not all these phases and characters are as easily dismissed or as clear cut as these three examples. So where did we go wrong? Presumably when we began to do things which each particular critic found unacceptable. So for Clifford Hill *et al.* it was the arrival of the Kansas City Prophets which sent the church into heresy;[3] Peter Glover goes further back to the whole 'Signs and Wonders' movement,[4] and James Jacob Prasch has a go at pretty much everything from Toronto to Alpha.[5] It will be worth taking a look at these three manifestations of this particular genre of book, since they are pretty similar in their methodology and style, even though some of their targets are slightly different. It would take a whole book the size of this one to attempt a detailed response, so instead I'll take a blanket look at the authors' methodology.

Prophetic voices?

The first thing to note is that the authors feel themselves to be prophetic voices of truth in a church which has lost the plot and is heading off into heresy and therefore judgement. Thus Philip Foster, in his preface to Prasch's book, says

The Churches today are in very deep trouble. That is the reason for this book. All around us are problems and errors, disillusionment and pain among Christians who had sought to follow the Lord by following their leaders. This book attempts to address these matters head on. If it is outspoken it is because someone must speak out when things are so bad.[6]

And Peter Glover asserts that

Those who hold to Scriptural truths, as the eternal and unchanging Word of God, are labelled 'nit-pickers', 'heresy hunters', and 'legalists' (for holding to doctrinal truths – what Jesus calls 'obeying my commandments'). The authors of this book would, no doubt, be described by some in this way for having the temerity to question them.[7]

Since his personal 'reformation', Mark Havill has

personally written to dozens of church leaders worldwide about unbiblical beliefs and practices connected with a faulty signs and wonders theology ... The reality appears to be that they do not love biblical truth and are leading countless thousands away from Bible-believing Christianity towards another gospel, another Jesus, and another Spirit![8]

The heresy which needs to be fought so courageously is, in each case, that the reformed evangelical church has abandoned the Word of God in scripture and gone off into various manifestations of wrong belief, bad practice and corrupt thinking. It is worth noting that this argument is therefore irrelevant to huge sections of the world-wide church, including Pentecostal and charismatic sections, which would have seen themselves as neither reformed nor evangelical in the first place, but then presumably that is evidence of even greater error on their part. However, we will stay with this debate since it is important in the British charismatic movement, many of whose members would say that they arrived within renewal from such a reformed position (some would even claim still to be there). Some of the writers of this genre would remain staunchly anti-charismatic, but most would be sympathetic to renewal as it was in the halcyon days before the particular heresy in question set in. But in any case their arguments are similar, and centre, as we've said, around the perceived abandoning of an evangelical approach to scripture.

The pattern of criticism

What of the methodology of these critics? Several tactics are in evidence to greater or lesser degrees in all the books in question. First of all there is a lumping together of some pretty diverse figures as being representative of whole movements. We have already noted the suspicion with which most British charismatics would regard the prosperity 'Word of Faith' movement. Yet in a book on exposing the 'Signs and Wonders' movement, there is a whole chapter devoted to the evils of the prosperity gospel. We have seen also the juxtaposition of John Wimber and Morris Cerullo in some critiques: I suppose that from the outside it is easy to see the two as bedfellows, but a more careful targeting would have made the critic's arguments more convincing. Any of us who heard Wimber speak regularly will remember all too clearly his extreme distaste for hype, manipulation and charlatanism in the healing ministry, and British listeners will have heard him apologize frequently for the fact that so much of it has emanated from his country. Charismatics could well listen to and learn from their critics if only they felt more fully understood and more accurately portrayed.

Second, since the church is in such very grave danger, the critics feel the need to name and shame the culprits. Their lists read like a *Who's Who* of church leadership from Augustine to Zwingli, and including such contemporary figures as John Arnott, Bill Bright, George Carey, Gerald Coates, Colin Dye, Roger and Faith Forster, Ken and Lois Gott, Nicky Gumbel, Jack Hayford, Tony Higton, Bill Hybels, Graham Kendrick, Sandy Millar, David Pytches, Mark Stibbe, Peter Wagner, David Yonggi Cho and, it goes without saying, John Wimber. I must admit to feeling slightly peeved, in a section of Prasch's book entitled 'Decline of the Anglican Charismatic Movement', not to get a mention myself!

145

At times the insults get personal, too. Colin Dye and others from Kensington Temple are mistaken over a point of practice: 'POPPYCOCK, the only thing [sic] in the heavenlies are their brains ... Someone needs to tell the Emperor [sic] he's wearing no clothes!'[9]

And even the Archbishop of Canterbury is not immune: 'When Satan has evangelicals like George Carey unwittingly in his service he needs no liberals.'[10]

But when there's so much at stake, such language, at the very least intemperate, is presumably OK.

Then, third, there is the employment of the logic which says that if you did anything wrong, or even silly, in the past, the rest of your ministry remains tainted by it, and it will also infect any others unfortunate enough to sit at your feet. So pages and pages have been used up as critics have delved about looking for links with suspect characters from the past in order to discredit current leaders.

Thus David Forbes examines the pedigree of Kansas City Prophet Paul Cain and finds that when young he sat at the feet of William Branham and was involved with the 'Latter Rain Movement'. Cain's teaching in 1990, when the KC prophets had their first major exposure in the UK, is shown to be exactly that of the 'Latter Rain' teachers and their closely linked allies the 'Manifest Sons of God' movement, which Forbes is certain was heretical. This allows him to write off the whole prophetic movement based around Kansas City as being doctrinally heretical, rather than just over-enthusiastic and a bit misguided, which is perhaps a more generous estimate ten years on. Similarly, the fact that Bob Jones, another of the KC prophets, had spent some time in a mental hospital and had previously led a somewhat unregenerate lifestyle means beyond question that he was demonized and was prophesying through an evil spirit.

I'd better come clean at this stage and admit a couple of dirty little secrets from my own past, so that you can write off this whole book. When I was at university I once smoked an illegal joint (just the once), and more recently I attended a meeting where Rodney Howard-Browne was speaking (again, just the once). I think that's just about all the sins I've ever committed, but they're all you need to prove conclusively that I am a heretic and that you shouldn't believe a word I say. So put the book down and go and do something useful instead.

The real point of all this is hidden in a little throwaway comment which one would either miss or accept blindly when reading through Hill's book. 'God can only use a purified people',[11] we're told, and it sounds a commendable enough comment. But the idea behind it is used throughout the book to sanction the quest for chinks in teachers' armour which will allow the writing off of whole swathes of their ministries and those of others associated with them, regardless of how much blessing may have come for how many people through them. We shall consider in a moment whether or not this premise is in fact true.

Fourth, there is the blanket condemnation of things in the church with which the authors do not agree. Alpha, for example, is 'fundamentally unscriptural', has a 'demonic aspect', and can never make disciples according to any biblical model because Alpha courses are not biblical.[12] 'The fact that so many churches ... are conducting their evangelism through the mechanism of the Alpha Course is not a cause for encouragement but for concern.' Some might think that the fact that the churches were conducting any evangelism at all is a cause for encouragement, but no: Alpha 'courts the risk of producing spurious conversions'.[13] 'Promise Keepers' is 'not of God' because it welcomes 'Mormons, Roman Catholics and non-evangelicals',[14] Rome is 'the harlot church',[15] Pensacola is 'All A Big Money Grabbing Con' (sic)[16], and charismatics in the Church of England (and their leaders) 'do not appear to have even the most elementary knowledge of the Word of God'.[17] But the greatest invective is saved for John Wimber himself: he is 'a true Gnostic': he and his followers are

> locusts who are destroying the church ... an evil force that God will totally exterminate. If someone wishes to be a part of a great army that God will lay waste, with its stench rising to the heavens, all they need to do is to join the Vineyard Fellowship.[18]

And so on. We could continue with this distasteful exercise, but I think you get the flavour.

Fifth, there is an attempt to explain away in quasi-scientific terms many of the more outrageous manifestations of some renewal gatherings. The Toronto Blessing of the mid-nineties clearly is a prime candidate for this kind of treatment. Philip Foster is quite careful in his use of the term 'hypnosis', claiming that charismatic meetings are attempts to hypnotize the crowd, but he loses credibility in moving on to talk about hysteria, which, as any psychiatrist will tell you, is the production of physical symptoms of illness which have no organic root by dis-ease in the mind. This misuse of pop-psychology by those who don't know what they are talking about is a common feature not just of the Sunday supplement writers, but also of those seeking to critique renewal at a more serious level.

But perhaps most seriously there are some fundamental biblical errors. This is serious indeed from authors who are accusing charismatics of letting go of scripture, or twisting its interpretation to suit their own ends. So, for example, the comment above that 'God can only use a purified people' is quite simply wrong. The clearest example is in Isaiah 45:1-6, where God announces his plans to use the pagan king Cyrus to fulfil his purpose for the release of his people from exile in Babylon, even though the king did not know God and had never acknowledged him. There is also the incident which John records for us in John 11:49-52 when Caiaphas the High Priest prophesies more than he knows about Jesus' death, apparently simply because of his role as High Priest. Far from being a rather nit-picky point, this piece of doctrine has vital implications for the church today.

As an Anglican liturgist I have watched with great interest the arrival of the *Common Worship* services which became legal at the end of the year 2000. One of the features of the new texts is their emphasis on God as Creator, an emphasis significant by its absence from earlier Anglican liturgies. What has happened to bring this element of biblical truth to the notice of the church? I believe that after 250 years of modernist culture, during which mankind has been 'the measure of all things' and the created world was seen as simply there for our convenience, to experiment on in the quest for new scientific truth or to abuse and destroy in the name of 'progress', we have finally heeded the voice of God through the Green movements, and listened to those whom many would want to write off as pagans who do not know or acknowledge God. They have managed to point out to Christians those bits of the Bible which show that God's redemptive purposes are for all of God's creation and not just people, just as two decades earlier the feminists reminded us that his purposes are for women as well as men. These truths had always been there in scripture, but we had looked at the Bible through our modernist spectacles and simply filtered out such passages as Romans 8:22ff. When the church begins to believe that it can only hear God's truth spoken to us through those who are 100 per cent doctrinally 'purified', we are in great danger. If all the 'light' is in here and all the 'darkness' out there, we close ourselves to the thoroughly biblical ways in which God might want to speak to us from outside the ghetto. But even more outrageous is the idea, upon which a whole chapter of Hill's book is built, that genuine prophecy is only ever miserable, and therefore that if a prophet speaks of blessing he is by definition out of order and therefore a false prophet.

It is important to note that God never sent prophets to Israel to announce blessing. He never sent his prophets to herald times of peace and prosperity. It was the false prophets who came with these messages.[19]

Which Bible is Hill reading from? Mine has sixteen chapters in the middle of the book of Isaiah which do exactly that, as the prophet speaks to a distressed and exiled people of God's plans to restore them to their own land amid great rejoicing. Similarly, sections of other prophetic books speak of the joy of restoration. It appears to be a tragic truth that if we give our minds too much to heresy-hunting they can easily become negative and doom-laden, thus making us prone to filtering out of our Bibles anything which speaks of grace, joy or restoration. And if only false prophets speak of good times to come, Hill himself must enter that camp with his promises of hope for the charismatic movement with which he ends his book.[20]

Finally there is a manipulative pressure to agree with the critics as having spoken and written from God. If you think they're wrong, you're wrong.

Some people will applaud me for having written this book, others will loathe me for it. Let God judge me as He sees fit; that is His responsibility. Yours is to ask Jesus to show you whether or not the things I have written are true ... I know that in writing this book I have done what God has required of me concerning these matters. It is before Him that I shall one day stand and have to give account for having written this book. It is before him that you will one day stand and give account for decisions you have made after having read it.[21]

One definition of manipulation is 'allowing the possibility of only one acceptable response to something'. I'm right, and if you pray and seek God hard enough you'll come to agree with me. And if you don't, you'll have to answer to God for it! The same attitude is to be found in Hill's appeal to all in the church, and especially leaders, to 'respond to the things we have written by examining their teaching and practices in the light of Scripture'.[22] Could it possibly be that many of us have done so already, and arrived at a position different from his? It is surely dangerous to suggest that until we've studied our Bibles to the point where we agree with what someone else says, we're just wrong.

How do we reply?

So what is going on here, and how might someone who feels positive about Alpha, Wimber and Toronto respond? Clearly the critics are on a crusade for Truth, which is of course highly commendable, but it seems tragically sad that this quest can at times appear to make them forget common politeness, friendly debate and moderation of language in dealing with fellow-Christians. As those who come generally from a reformed evangelical position, whether or not they would claim to be charismatics too, they are looking for absolutes: absolute doctrinal orthodoxy, absolute integrity in the lives of those they attack, absolute purity of practice. So the mistakes, silly pronouncements and horror stories of their 'opponents' give them ammunition which can help them discount not just individuals but whole movements. The case against is proven if just one flaw can be found. There seems tragically to be no understanding of the biblical fact that anyone's ministry will be a mixture of good and bad, successes and mistakes, orthodoxy and heresy. God, who does show grace and forgiveness, is still able to use fallen, sinful or just plain silly people, as the Bible bears eloquent witness.

So yes, of course the Toronto Blessing was a mixture of human and divine activity, which had its excesses and silliness. Of course Alpha is not 100 per cent perfect as an evangelistic tool; of course some exponents of 'Signs and Wonders' are a bit misguided at times. And yes, the Docklands conference in 1990 does with the benefit of hindsight seem to have been a big mistake, in all sorts of ways. But whether or not that means that the whole renewal movement is a satanically inspired deception, or even that it has terminally lost its way, is surely open to debate.

That's why it is so difficult to enter into debate with people who take the kind of approach we've been looking at: we're not starting from the same place, or even playing on the same field. My Bible seems to suggest to me that God works with people on the way towards maturity, purity and orthodoxy. Theirs seems rather to say that if you get anything even a bit wrong you're a demonic deceiver. And, of course, if you disagree with us you're even more so, and will one day be judged for it. It is very difficult to enter into constructive argument with those who feel themselves to be 100 per cent right and have God to back them up! Sadly, any attempt at debate can easily degenerate into the kind of invective which we have sampled above.

However, just because we might not like the style and tone of these attacks on some bits of renewal, we still need the maturity to listen anyway, lest there is some truth in their content. Has renewal in fact taken the church off the rails and away from scripture? Can the manifestations of renewal, especially the more dramatic ones witnessed during the Toronto Blessing phase, be explained in terms of psychology and sociology alone, without any reference to the Holy Spirit? And is it true that 'the leaders of the charismatic movement in the Church of England are by and large doctrinally ignorant men who are uneducated in their knowledge and understanding of the scriptures God gave us to protect us from deception?'[23] Is this true across the denominational spectrum?

The psychological question is an important one, since any religious experience happens at the interface between God, our own minds and bodies, and the group of which we're a part. Mature charismatics have learnt not to be afraid of the critiques of psychologists and sociologists, particularly those with no particular axe to grind other than understanding what is going on. A book called, rather unhelpfully, *The Toronto Blessing – or Is It?*[24] which looks from its cover as if it belongs to the same stable as Prasch, Glover and the rest, is actually a very helpful collection of essays by a sociologist and theologian, a psychiatrist, a historian and a worship musician, each giving their angle on Toronto, and being pretty positive about it, too. In another book, medical doctor Patrick Dixon puts the manifestations down to 'altered states of consciousness', but unlike Philip Foster, who reaches the same conclusion, he sees nothing sinister at all in this.[25] He quotes Simon Wessley, senior lecturer in the medical school at King's College, London (my old college, and therefore by definition infallible!):

> This religious experience appears to be cathartic. The people feel rather good about it and appear to go for the purpose of group ecstatic experience. It is not mass hysteria or any form of mental disorder – it may be rather un-English, but there is nothing sinister about it at all.[26]

Nigel Scotland agrees, and argues in his refutation of Foster's chapter that anyway hypnotism may not always be a bad thing, a position which will no doubt do nothing to endear him to the reformed evangelical critics of renewal, but which nevertheless seems manifestly good sense to me.

Have we lost the plot ... or discovered more of it?

But what about the deeper issue of biblical apostasy? Have charismatics lost the plot? Well, it depends on your point of view. It is certainly true that charismatic renewal has bitten deeply into the reformed evangelical camp as people have discovered a gospel of power and experience rather than one they would, with hindsight, view as having been about words alone. Charismatics often speak also of having discovered a gospel of grace rather than condemnation. Some no doubt feel liberated by their charismatic experience from such a position, but it is easy to see how those who remain within that camp might view their erstwhile colleagues as having gone off the rails. For many reformed evangelicals, charismatic renewal is a scary threat to the orthodoxy of the church, not least because it is so demonstrably successful. But to others who might believe that reformed evangelicalism is itself an unscriptural position to hold, the angry and at times vicious arguments cause great sadness rather than any change of position. The invective can and should act as a reminder to charismatics that we do need to monitor carefully our beliefs and practices in the light of the way we understand the Bible, and that at times we even need to repent of past mistakes. But generally charismatics would not be swayed by attacks such as these, and would only be saddened by their tone. And personally I would find it very hard to put into print stinging condemnations of godly men and women who may not be perfect but who will go down in history as those who have shaped the church at the turn of this millennium, won thousands to Christ, and prayed and laboured for the renewing of the church and the saving of the world. I could not condemn those who have achieved far more for the kingdom in any single week of their life than I will in the entirety of mine, even if I don't see eye to eye with them on every point of doctrine. I'm happy to stick with Sandy Millar, Graham Kendrick and the rest: it somehow feels safer. It certainly feels nicer, and at the end of the day more biblical, too.

So without a detailed refutation of their arguments, that is my view, and that of many other charismatics, on these kinds of attacks. To abandon the reformed evangelical faith in favour of charismatic renewal is only a move into major apostasy if you first accept the view that the reformed evangelical faith is the one and only Truth. However, if you believe that, like any other doctrinal position, it is likely to contain some truth mixed up with a degree of blindness, to move out of it will seem less like losing the plot than discovering a bit more of it. I may, of course, be wrong and mistaken, but that isn't likely, so if you disagree with me, well, you'll have to answer to the Almighty yourself for that. But I'll tell you this: I wouldn't want to be in your shoes on that great and terrible day!

Keeping the tea hot

However, there is one more subject we need briefly to address before we close this chapter. John Finney is a retired Anglican bishop who is very much in favour of charismatic renewal, but nevertheless asks questions about the life of the charismatic movement as a movement within the church. His basic question is stated thus: why do cups of tea always become lukewarm? 'The second law of thermodynamics is depressing. It says that things wear out, become more alike, distinctions disappear ... Things tend to become more bland, less different, more ordinary.'[27]

He observes that, traditionally, renewal movements have seemed to obey the same law, losing momentum and eventually running out of steam. Is this true of current charismatic renewal? Finney wonders whether as a movement it might have peaked, not because it has gone off the rails but because movements do peak, as a simple matter of sociology. All that is left is fading splendour.

Like all good postmodernists he does some of his theology through the medium of story, and he tells the tale of a family whose rebellious teenagers increasingly question the values of their parents and become involved with eco-warriors. The end of the story is left up to us to construct out of several possible alternatives: the youngsters might eventually kill themselves on drug overdoses or ruin their lives with pregnancies and abortions, or the eco-warriors might realize that less direct confrontation and more political action might serve their ends better. Alternatively, the very political parties which had fought the warriors might become affected by them and gradually embrace more environment-friendly policies. The kids might end up doing forestry degrees and going to plant trees in Brazil.

This parable suggests different ways in which renewal movements within the church might end up, either in heresy and disorder, in relatively peaceful co-existence, or by joining the establishment, but affecting it for the good as they do so. Finney then traces four historic renewal movements: the renewal of Judaism by Jesus and his followers in the first century, the founding of the monastery at Cluny in the tenth century, the European Reformation, and the two American Awakenings of the eighteenth and nineteenth centuries. Each of these movements eventually came to an end as a specific movement, but they have all continued to influence the church in very different ways. Finney suggests some reasons for the fading splendour, and then turns his attention to the contemporary charismatic scene. Has this renewal movement peaked, and is there nothing left but fading splendour?

Finney concludes:

> I think that, from our examination of the facts, we have to accept that renewals inevitably change and appear to lose their intensity ... there seems almost to be a spiritual requirement that renewals will change and lose their focus.[28]

So what do we do about it? Here Finney's perceptive wisdom shines out most clearly, I believe. He suggests first a principle, and then three practicalities in the light of his investigations: 'It is seldom sensible to fight against reality, for sooner or later it rebounds vindictively. Castles in the sky hurt people when they fall ... Playing "Let's pretend" is not an option.'[29]

Therefore, he suggests, those involved in the leadership of any kind of renewal movement should first of all avoid nostalgia and the very natural desire to get back to how things were in the beginning. Our focus should be the future, not the past. Second, we should not try to fight the natural bureaucratization, but do it as well and as efficiently as we can. And third, we should broaden out our aims from the initial often single-issue emphasis around which we started. There is more to renewal than baptism in the Holy Spirit! To these three I would want to add a fourth of my own, based on the thinking of Graham Cray which we touched on in the previous chapter: we should, I believe, continue to look for and expect the action of God which is not in a continuum with the past but which represents a new inbreaking of his sovereign will.

Finney's perceptive wisdom needs close attention. Maybe the 'charismatic movement' has peaked, but my response to that is to say that I am in no way arguing for the continuance of a movement for its own sake, but that the church rediscovers as a basic ingredient of Christian discipleship the functional reality of the Holy Spirit. Finney distinguishes between 'strand A', renewal which hives off from the mainstream and becomes a separate sect or denomination, and 'strand B' renewal, which stays in close touch and therefore influences the mainstream, while inevitably losing some of its own distinctiveness in the process. In the current scene the New Churches represent strand A, while an organization like Anglican Renewal Ministries represents strand B. Finney draws the conclusion from his research that at the end of the day strand B achieves more of lasting value and affects the whole church scene much more than does strand A, but then as an Anglican bishop you might expect him to say that! However, if the insights of forty years of charismatic renewal can become assimilated into the church and once again become normative, after centuries of either belonging solely to a small fringe or being lost entirely, the movement will have done its job and needs no longer to exist as a movement. I hope that is the way it is, and I hope that you will have seen this book not as something arguing for a particular party within the church, but for the spirituality which that party has worked hard to get back on to the agenda.

Well, that's about enough arguing for one book. I've tried to explain what renewal is all about, and why I think it is so important. I've tried to take seriously some of the arguments of its opponents, and to prove my central thesis that being charismatic is not an option – it's a command. So where does that leave us? I'm going on to suggest that we need to make a personal response, but first, after so many objections, let's take a look at charismatic renewal in action. If it really is how we were always meant to be Christians, we'd expect to see some degree of health and success in churches which have embraced it gladly. Does it really make a difference? Let's see!

Part Four

Making a
Difference

Chapter 16

If You Can't Beat 'Em ...

Well, that's the theory. Let's now look at renewal in action, and see if it really does make a difference. I'll begin by examining the success of charismatic churches.

I've already touched on this briefly, of course, in an earlier chapter, but I need to put more flesh on the bare bones of the assertion I slipped in without any proof. I also need to remind you that I am looking at the church on a world-wide scale, and that the British church (in fact most of the church in Western Europe and North America) is not the best example at which to look. Anyway, let's begin with the facts.

The growth of pentecostal spirituality

One problem with gathering information about the charismatic movement is that you can't easily see it all. New Testament scholar Mark Bonnington makes the point that charismatic spirituality is a 'plug-and-play' spirituality in that you can attach it to other, perhaps more easily identifiable movements within the church.[1] It is relatively easy to gain information about, for example, how many Baptists there are in England, how many Methodists or Roman Catholics. It is also fairly easy to identify membership of different parties within my church, the Church of England: there are x Anglo-Catholics, y Evangelicals, and so on. But charismatics aren't so easily counted, since they belong to all of the denominations and most of the parties within the church. It really is much harder to get hold of them all to count them.

Nevertheless, in spite of these difficulties, David Barrett and Todd Johnson attempt each year to obtain statistics which are as reliable as possible, and their category of 'Pentecostal/charismatic', which they admit overlaps considerably with their denominational breakdown, forms the basis for these figures from January 2000.

Consider first of all these statistics of the population of the world from the beginning of the twentieth century, projected to 2025:[2]

1900	1,619,886,800
1970	3,696,148,000
1990	5,226,442,000
2000	6,055,049,000
2025	7,823,703,000

How many of these are Christians? This table tells us:

1900	558,056,300	that is, 34.4% of the world population
1970	1,236,314,000	that is, 33.4%
1990	1,747,462,000	that is, 33.4%
2000	1,999,566,000	that is, 38.2%
2025	2,616,670,000	that is, 33.4%

So for the last hundred years or so, about a third of the world's population would call themselves Christians, a figure which is not projected to change much in the immediate future. But now look at the growth of the Pentecostal denominations during this time:

	Pentecostals/ charismatics	Percentage of world population	Percentage of all Christians
1900	3,700,000	0.23%	0.66%
1970	72,223,000	1.95%	5.84%
1990	425,486,000	8.14%	24.34%
2000	523,727,000	8.65%	26.19%
2025	811,522,000	10.37%	31.01%

What this means is that Pentecostalism grew in a hundred years from representing less than 1 per cent of the world-wide church to representing over a quarter. Note in particular the meteoric rise between 1970 and the end of the century, a growth in thirty years of 451.5 million people, or over 15 million per year. Statistician Peter Brierley comments: 'This phenomenal growth is unprecedented for any other group in world-wide Christianity'[3] Commenting specifically on the area of most powerful growth within the Pentecostal denominations, he adds,

> To grow from 2.6 million in 1960 in South America to over 58 million 50 years later is a story of God's amazing grace in a nutshell ... In the decade of the 80s 42 million Pentecostals in those ten years joined the 46 million at the start of that decade. Certainly not in recent history, and maybe never since the first century, have proportionally so many joined a church in so short a period in so many continents.[4]

Of course, it can be argued that these kinds of statistics are only vaguely accurate, since many who would claim to be Christians might have only minimal awareness of the gospel or its meaning. You have only to look at nominal Catholicism in many European countries and nominal Anglicanism in England to see this principle. But the rate of nominality within renewal is considerably lower, by its very nature, so that argument only pushes the proportions even higher. Clearly there is something in this spirituality which works!

The dramatic growth of pentecostal spirituality led theologian Harvey Cox to investigate its nature in his book *Fire from Heaven.*[5] Over thirty years ago he wrote a bestseller called *The Secular City*[6] which was, in his own words, an attempt

> to work out a theology for the 'postreligious' age that many sociologists had assured us was coming. Since then, however, religion – or at least some religions – seems to have gained a new lease of life. Today it is secularity, not spirituality, that may be headed for extinction.[7]

What had made the difference? The main answer was the dramatic and unprecedented growth of pentecostalism. Cox began his journey of investigation because

> it had become obvious that instead of the 'death of God' some theologians pronounced not many years ago, or the waning of religion that sociologists had extrapolated, something quite different had taken place ... a religious renaissance of sorts is under way all over the globe.[8]

For this renewal to have turned round the heart and mind of a hardened academic theologian who was preparing for the death of Christianity must say something about its divine power!

The 'New Church' movement

But what of the charismatic churches outside the Pentecostal denominations? As I said, statistics are not easy to get hold of, but one area we can look at fairly easily is the growth of the British 'New Churches', which I mentioned briefly earlier on. Formerly they were called 'House Churches' but felt it right to change the name when most of them grew too large to continue meeting in houses. Now that most of them are over thirty years old it might be about time they changed their name again!

Nobody intended to found a new denomination, of course.[9] It was just that frustrated charismatics who were not allowed to express their new-found spirituality within the life of their existing churches began to meet in one another's houses for the kind of worship and fellowship they craved. After a while they began to do that instead of going along on a Sunday morning, either because they didn't see why they should put up with what felt increasingly like 'dead' traditional worship, or in some cases because they had felt hounded out of their churches. The 'services' were in the old days minimalist: lots of sung worship, sharing from the Bible, perhaps an informal 'breaking of bread' and prayer for one another. But the new-found faith of these early charismatics and their evangelistic zeal meant that they began to attract others, many from their previous churches or others like them, but also some from outside the church scene altogether.

Of course, it was inevitable that the House Churches should go the way of all flesh, into bureaucracy. The typical New Church today would be part of a large 'stream' (denomination, really) into which the hundreds of small independent fellowships have coalesced. They would meet in a school hall or gym, or perhaps a pub or community centre which they rented out each Sunday. There would be a denominational HQ somewhere, with paid staff to run it, and increasingly there are the equivalents of theological colleges to train new leaders. And once a year there would be the denominational knees-ups at Bible Weeks or Revival Camps, where the faithful would gather for teaching, celebration and ministry, and to be inspired and re-envisioned for the task ahead.

But all this organization has done little to blunt the charismatic and evangelistic cutting edge of the New Churches, and their growth has been astronomic.

To the different streams or 'Tribes' of the New Churches must be added a significant development when at the end of the 1980s the first British Vineyard Fellowship was planted. John Wimber had said that he had no plans to colonize Britain with his denomination, but when John Mumford, an Anglican priest who had spent some time with John over in Anaheim at the Vineyard HQ, felt the call of God to plant a church in London, John Wimber agreed that it was indeed God's call for him, and the colonization began. The first Vineyard Fellowship, in southwest London, began under John Mumford's leadership, and others soon followed. By 1999 there were 59 Vineyards in the British Isles, and a significant number of them are led by men who are, like John Mumford, ex-Anglican clergy. They seem to be enjoying growth and success in most places. But more significantly, the penetration of Vineyard style and values into the Church of England through Wimber conferences and the New Wine Network has been dramatic.

So how does their garden grow? Although they still represent only a small proportion of all British Christians, the New Churches have seen the most dramatic increase in numbers of any denomination or grouping, in fact the only real growth at all in Britain. After literally starting from scratch in the late sixties, they grew rapidly to their present membership of 200,000. In the decade of the eighties alone they grew by 144 per cent, from 44,400 to 108,500. Commenting on their go-getting style and refusal to be trapped by outdated traditions, Peter Brierley imagines

> their motto might easily have been that of Hannibal when facing the Pyrenees on his elephants, 'I will find a way across or make one'. They were determined to make the Kingdom of God relevant, and literally tens of thousands of people in England have joined their churches.[10]

Of course, as many accusations have suggested, a certain amount of this growth was transfer growth from other Christian denominations, but that simply reinforces my point: thousands of people are leaving dead or dying churches with little sense of the power and presence of God, and at least some of them are finding satisfying new spiritual life within the charismatic renewal. Again, the growth statistics suggest that something here works.

Church growth guru Peter Wagner agrees:

> Any careful observer visiting churches internationally would know for certain that the considerable majority of committed Christians worldwide would be regarded as part of the Pentecostal-charismatic stream ... My research has led me to make this bold statement: *In all of human history, no other non-political, non-militaristic, voluntary human movement has grown as rapidly as the Pentecostal-charismatic movement in the last 25 years.*[11]

Growth among Roman Catholics

One of the most fascinating areas of growth in the charismatic movement is that among Roman Catholics. In a deeply prophetic examination of the recent fate of his church, American Catholic writer Ralph Martin asks why it is the case that in every continent of the world, and not just Latin America, the Catholic Church is losing members hand over fist to what he calls 'Protestant Pentecostal sects'.[12] He quotes statistic after statistic to demonstrate both the decline of commitment to his own church and the growth of the Pentecostal churches, and draws out from it a dramatic conclusion: what people are looking for in their religion is conversion to Jesus and an experience of the Holy Spirit. They are searching, in short, for the presence of God. Martin goes on to study those few Catholic churches which are bucking the trend and growing: his conclusion is that there is growth in the Catholic Church only where there is emphasis on a personal relationship with Jesus Christ as Lord and Saviour, and baptism in the Holy Spirit as normative Christian experience. Unless the whole of the Roman Church begins to embrace these aspects of spirituality, argues Martin, there is little hope for the future other than continuing decline and death.

Among the welter of scholars and churchmen whom he quotes is Pope John Paul II, speaking to the massed bishops of Latin America in 1992, and calling passionately for 'a new evangelization':

What will free us from these signs of death? ... Christ is the only one who can free us from this evil ... It makes the task that the church is facing more urgent: to rekindle in the heart of all the baptized the grace they received. 'I remind you,' St Paul wrote to Timothy, 'to stir into flame the gift that you have.'

Just as the people of the new covenant received life through the Holy Spirit at Pentecost, only this acceptance will raise up a people capable of giving birth to men and women who are renewed and free, and conscious of their dignity ...

Today the Lord is passing by. He is calling you. In this moment of grace he is once again calling you by name and renewing his covenant with you. May you listen to his voice.[13]

Two leading Roman scholars, Fr Kilian McDonnell (whom we have already mentioned) and Fr George Montague, demonstrate a clear link between this new evangelization and the work of the Holy Spirit in charismatic renewal. After studying the first eight centuries of the history of the church, they conclude that baptism in the Holy Spirit should be the norm for Christians: 'Accepting the baptism in the Spirit is not joining a movement ... Rather it is embracing the fullness of Christian initiation, which belongs to the church.'[14]

Martin explains: 'What we are talking about here is something as fundamental as conversion, as what the New Testament describes as normal Christian life, as starting out with a "full deck".'[15] And it is happening. Martin estimates that 72 million Roman Catholics have experienced charismatic renewal, and that this spiritual renewal has brought renewal to many other areas of their churches' lives.

Quality as well as quantity

But is it enough to say that three-quarters of a billion Pentecostals can't be wrong? Size isn't everything, and the sheer numbers of people involved in something don't necessarily make it right; you only have to look at how many people read the *Sun*! There's plenty of quantity in renewal, but is there any quality? The answer is an unequivocal 'Yes!'

Come with me to a typical charismatic church for its Sunday morning service. It doesn't particularly matter which denomination we visit: much of the feel of the service would be pretty similar wherever. And as you come with me, imagine that you are a first-time visitor who has only previously attended church for weddings and funerals. You will no doubt bring with you all sorts of presuppositions and fantasies about what you are in for, expecting a dark gloomy atmosphere, ancient hymns in archaic language wheezed out by an asthmatic organ and an organist who looks as if she's got one foot in the grave and the other on a banana skin. You will probably be scared because you don't know the rules: when should I stand up or kneel down; which book do I use and on which page; will I get thrown out or at least glared at if my baby so much as burps?

But your immediate reaction as you enter the church is likely to be one of colour, brightness and buzz. You will be greeted warmly but sensitively at the door, and as you find a seat you will be smiled at and not glared at by others. You're impressed with the numbers of men, young people and children present: you'd thought that church was only for old ladies. As the service begins there is an air of informality, and the stiff, starchy unfriendliness which you were expecting isn't in evidence at all. The singing moves from exuberant praise into intimate reverence and back again, the teaching is

Bible-based and really does seem to connect with life on *your* planet, and some kind of a response to it is expected and catered for, perhaps with the offer of personal prayer ministry. You didn't find the service easy, and you didn't really know any of the songs, except that lovely gentle one they do on *Songs of Praise* sometimes, which you did enjoy, but you could see very clearly that everyone else was having a good time. There was a kind of uncomfortable comfortableness about the service, and once or twice, much to your surprise and for no explicable reason, you found yourself filling up a bit, although you don't think anyone noticed.

At home afterwards you have a look at the notice-sheet which you were given as you went in. It reveals a wealth of mid-week activities including various projects to reach out to and care for people in the community, homegroups for study and support, and perhaps an evangelistic 'Alpha', 'Emmaus' or 'Saints Alive!' course, designed for people like you who are newcomers. But would you go back? You have to admit there's something going on there. You're not sure what it is, but you suppose it's what they would call 'God'. There was definitely something in the atmosphere which felt a bit scary at times, but scary in a nice way, if you know what I mean. It certainly was nowhere near as awful as you'd expected it to be. Yes, all in all, you might give it another go sometime.

What you would not see as a first-time visitor is that the financial giving is substantially above the average, the leadership is typically visionary, and the congregation has a sense of purpose: they are going somewhere together. They are probably going there along with other like-minded churches in the area, too. Church life is anything but a holy huddle and more of the same.

An idealized picture, of course, and no doubt you'll easily be able to come up with some stories of charismatic churches you have visited which were anything but so pleasant. But this picture is not so idealized that it bears no relation at all to reality. Charismatic churches are likely to be at the forefront of vision, every-member ministry and evangelism, providing of course that they are charismatic as a matter of church policy, and are being led by leaders who are unashamedly taking them in that direction. After all, to grow as dramatically as they are growing must mean that something about them is attractive.

167

Burning with the flame of the Spirit

So what picture overall do these objective statistics and subjective impressions give us? They point to a set of churches which are unmistakably growing, showing that there is something about them which is deeply attractive to people. Should that surprise us? Surely not. The Holy Spirit was given by the Father to the church to empower it for witness, so that men, women and children could to come to Christ to find a personal relationship with him, sins forgiven, lives healed and relationships restored. Shouldn't it be the case then that churches with a greater awareness of the Holy Spirit, a greater understanding of his work and a greater degree of openness to his leading and guiding are the very churches most likely to benefit from the fruits of his presence? It seems obvious that a group of Christians whose own spirituality and experience of God really has made a difference to them will be the most likely ones to want to share the good news enthusiastically with others. Nigel Scotland, commenting on the accusation that charismatics are introversionist, with little concern for evangelism, asserts instead that

> Some of the most effective evangelising churches in the nation are charismatic. Cobham Christian Fellowship, Kensington Temple, Holy Trinity Brompton, St Michael-le-Belfry, York, Millmead Baptist Church, Guildford, St Thomas Crookes, Sheffield, and Clarendon Church in Hove immediately come to mind. Taken as a whole, statistics demonstrate conclusively that charismatic churches are the most effective evangelizers.[16]

Cult writer Terry Pratchett makes this point wonderfully in *Carpe Jugulum*, one of his famous Discworld novels, and comments with his characteristic perceptive humour on the tragic uselessness of much of the church. Circumstances have thrown Granny Weatherwax, an atheistic witch, together with the Quite Reverend Mightily Oats, a priest of the god Om.

> 'It'd be as well for you if I didn't believe,' she said, prodding him with a sharp finger. 'This Om ... anyone seen him?'

'It is said three thousand people witnessed his manifestation at the Great Temple when he made the Covenant with the prophet Brutha and saved him from death by torture on the Iron Turtle –'

'But I bet that now they're arguing about *what* they actually saw, eh?'

'Well, indeed, yes, there are many opinions –'

'Right. Right. That's people for you. Now if *I'd* seen him, really there, really alive, it'd be in me like a fever. If I thought there was some god who really did care two hoots about people, who watched 'em like a father and cared for 'em like a mother ... well, you wouldn't catch me sayin' things like "There are two sides to every question," and "We must respect other people's beliefs." You wouldn't find *me* just being gen'rally nice in the hope that it'd all turn out right in the end, not if that flame was burning in me like an unforgivin' sword. And I did say burnin', Mr Oats, 'cos that's what it'd be. You say that you people don't burn folks and sacrifice people any more, but that's what true faith would mean, y'see? Sacrificin' your own life, one day at a time, to the flame, declarin' the truth of it, workin' for it, breathin' the soul of it. *That's* religion. Anything else is just ... is just bein' nice. And a way of keeping in touch with the neighbours.'

She relaxed slightly, and went on in a quieter voice: 'Anyway, that's what I'd be, if I really believed. And I don't think that's fashionable right now, 'cos it seems that if you sees evil now you have to wring your hands and say, "Oh deary me, we must debate this." '[17]

Who but those with the flame of the Holy Spirit burning within them ought to be the greatest evangelists in the church? The facts suggest that this is really the case.

Working for unity

But renewal doesn't stop with individual Christians or individual churches. Another area in which charismatics have rewritten the rule book is that of ecumenism. I have referred in a somewhat tongue-in-cheek way to the suspicion with which Christians regarded those from other branches of the church in the long-ago days of my youth, and tremendous strides forward have been made since then by the ecumenical movement. All sorts of councils, conversations and agreements have brought different bits of the Body of Christ together, so that apart from on the extreme edges, suspicion has all but died. We really do believe, most of us, that Christians who happen to go to another sort of church genuinely are the real thing, and that we almost certainly will be sharing heaven with them eventually. But in spite of all the talk, very little progress has been made towards what the ecumaniacs call 'visible unity'. I may now believe that Methodists are real Christians after all, and that is a tremendous step forward, but the fact remains that for the moment they are still Methodists and I am still an Anglican.

But if this 'top-down' kind of ecumenism has made great strides forward, there is another kind, which is much more 'bottom-up', which is working for a different kind of unity, and with a high degree of success. Let me tell you the story of the city I worked in, not because it is that special, but because it is the situation I know best. I know also, though, that this picture is being replicated in cities all over Britain.

It began with one Anglican vicar who had on him what we later recognized as an 'apostolic' anointing for the city. In other words, God had given him a ministry wider than just his own church and parish, and a desire to see different churches working together across the city for prayer and evangelism. His somewhat entrepreneurial character meant that he could start things up and make them happen in a way which invited others to join him. He began to meet with a few other leaders in whom he recognized a kindred spirit, and when I moved into the city I was invited to join this group. We didn't have a name, although my wife christened us in a somewhat tongue-in-cheek way 'The Magnificent Seven', a name which stuck, never in public but as a piece of shorthand for the group itself. Three of us were Anglicans, two were Baptists, and two were from a New Church.

At first we met simply to pray for the city and for each other, and these growing and deepening relationships were of tremendous value to me during the difficult early years in my parish, as they were to a couple of the others who were similarly facing difficult times. But after a while we felt convicted that the love and unity we shared was something to be shed further abroad in the city. First of all we gathered a few key people from the churches we represented to share our vision of greater co-operation, a meeting which was exciting and which felt like the start of something much bigger. Gradually we became aware of God's call to go both wider and deeper, and we took the radical step of deciding that one week we would all cancel our evening services and meet together.

The first such 'City Celebration' was held in an ancient monastery which we rented from the council. It housed a museum downstairs and a meeting room upstairs, and we attracted about 120 people as well as the powerful presence of the Spirit of God. We decided it was worth doing again, and began a monthly pattern, but soon we were attracting about 200 people and we outgrew that venue.

The next biggest place was my church, which was a beautiful building and ideal for that kind of an event. It seated 250, but within a few months we had grown to 400 and so had to move on again, this time to another Anglican church in the city centre. By now about 35 different churches around the city had become involved, and the 'Magnificent Seven' had to change its unofficial name as more and more leaders attended. When City Celebration reached 800 people, we moved into the cathedral. On one memorable occasion our charismatic diocesan bishop came and celebrated Holy Communion for us. At a special meeting a few weeks ago, I heard that the 2,000-seater cathedral had been crammed with over 3,100 people. (If you're a fire officer, that's just a rumour. I wasn't there, OK?)

But this wasn't just about nice meetings for Christians. Barriers were broken down between the congregations as they learnt to love and trust those from other churches. The relationships between their leaders trickled down so that there were deepening relationships on the ground, too. All kinds of prayer initiatives and evangelistic projects were generated, and the church began not just to work as one, but more importantly to think of itself as one. People would tell you that they belonged to the Christian church in that city, but that on Sunday mornings they went to this or that particular congregation of it.

Another important breakthrough was made when a liberal Catholic Anglican canon was invited to speak at a City Celebration.

Very movingly he told of the pain he felt at being excluded from something God was obviously at work through because he could not easily embrace its charismatic style. From then on specific attempts were made to build bridges and to be sensitive to those from other traditions, without compromising the Spirit-led ethos of the group.

That all began over ten years ago. Leaders came and went, me included, but the work goes on. The original visionary leader has gone off to be a bishop, but the 'apostolic' vision has passed on to someone else. There's a buzz in the air in that city, and in others like it, and an awareness that God is powerfully at work, commanding his blessing where brothers and sisters live together in unity. No agreements have been signed, no two denominations have coalesced into one, no committees forge joint statements or doctrinal positions, but Christians love one another, and are working together as well as apart for the kingdom of God. This is ecumenism, Jim, but not as we know it.

A book which became very significant for us along the way tells of the revival in Argentina, and the ways in which the churches worked together there.[18] We soon realized that what God was leading us into had much in common with Ed Silvoso's strategy for taking whole cities for God, and we sought to learn from his much more developed strategy. His book became an important guide for the journey towards unity and co-operation.

Renewal spirituality and the postmodern world

So charismatic/pentecostal spirituality does seem to have been, so far, a pretty successful way to believe and to do church. But what of the future? It is only a relatively new movement (if you forget the New Testament and the early church, of course): has it any future? Well, as Harvey Cox discovered, you never can tell, but I believe there is one more factor which makes charismatic spirituality's prospects for the future look good. Mike Riddell makes this point in his *Threshold of the Future*,[19] and in a nutshell it is to do with that cultural shift we have already described as a move from modernism to postmodernism and the end of the unquestioned reign of science as god. Riddell points out the similarities between Evangelicalism and modernism, where the approach to the Bible was essentially 'scientific'. In Evangelical spirituality it is treated as a textbook which contains a set body of knowledge, which, if we study it enough, will yield up its 'biblical principles' so that we may live correctly. He notes the amazing growth of Evangelicalism during the modernist period, with the Great Awakening, the Wesleyan Revivals and so on, and suggests that this was in part due to the way in which Evangelicalism chimed in with the spirit of the age.

But now that modernism is all but dead, a new culture has emerged. Postmodernism is much more to do with experienced truth than dogma given by some authority figure; it is more interested in community than in setting boundary markers to keep others out; it values authenticity more than set beliefs; it asks not 'Is this true?' but rather 'Does this work?' Now which sort of spirituality works with experienced authenticity mediated through a community? Which spirituality wants faith to make a real difference, here and now, to my life? Which seeks an awesome encounter with the living God more than dry truths preached from a book? There is something in renewal spirituality which I believe connects with a postmodern world where people are on a quest for something more than the church's tired dogmas, where people are welcome to belong in the hope that further down the track they might believe, rather than being told they must believe before they can really belong. In short, I believe that renewal is a God-given opportunity for his church to reach a lost world looking for anything which will help them find meaning in life. Does that mean we don't need the Bible and Christian doctrine any more? Of course not: we need them even more, like we've never needed them before. The road ahead is a risky one, with all sorts of fake spiritualities on offer, waiting to lead people off down a side-track and wanting to pervert the revealed truth of the Christian gospel if they possibly can. But a church which buries its head in the sand and sticks on the safe ground of old ways of believing in order to protect itself from possible error will find in time that it has also protected itself successfully from the real world out there and from any possibility of winning more than a few people from it. The future, I firmly believe, is bright: the future's charismatic.

All of which leaves me with one agonized question: why can't all churches see that renewal works and get on board? This isn't the right place for me to bang on about one of my hobby-horses, but it seems absolutely ludicrous to me that any non-charismatic churches continue to exist, given the dramatic success of renewal world-wide. But because we find it embarrassing, or convince ourselves that it doesn't quite match up to our pet interpretation of the Bible, or for whatever other reasons, we plod along, to all intents and purposes excluding the work of the Holy Spirit from our lives and our churches, or at the very least limiting what he does to the normal, natural and predictable, in spite of the welter of evidence suggesting that to do so will lead to decay and death. Our death wish is incredible, and it isn't just about us. How many millions of people are losing touch with church, or have lost it altogether, because some of us on the inside find the kind of church which would stand a statistically more significant chance of winning them not quite our thing? Why on earth don't more of our church leaders wake up, seek out some charismatics and say to them 'For God's sake, tell me what you've got that I haven't! What have you done to get your church to grow?' But no, that would be just too difficult to do. Who knows what might happen if we went down that route? I might lose control – that's probably the bottom line for many leaders. So we invent lots of clever excuses as to why we're declining, like 'remnant' theology and 'search' theology and 'Of course it's very hard in *my* parish' theology and 'We're called to faithfulness not success' theology. Who are they trying to kid? WAKE UP CHURCH! THIS CAN WORK! GET ON BOARD WITH RENEWAL! Sorry. End of sermon.

Chapter 17

For the Sake of the Children

Anglican Renewal Ministries, the organization for which I currently work, ran a conference a few years ago entitled 'Empowering Youth', to help clergy and youth leaders in their ministry among teenagers. We began the conference on a sober note, with a liturgy of lament (which subsequently became known as the 'Lentil Liturgy') in which we mourned the phenomenal drop-off of children and youth from the church. The high (or low) spot of the service was the pouring out on the altar of lentils, one to represent each child or young person lost from the church over the previous twenty years. This pouring out took nearly 15 minutes, as 38 people processed to the front in silence, each with a milk bottle full of mung beans, and poured them into a large tank. By the time we'd finished, there were 907,000 beans in the tank, and quite a few teardrops on the floor, too. I reminded the delegates that these beans represented only those youngsters who had once been in churches and had now left: there were, of course, plenty more who had never had anything to do with church in the first place. It seems too obvious to say that whatever it is that the church has been doing with its children, it hasn't been working.

The 'Father Christmas Syndrome'

It is my conviction that one significant reason for this drop-off is the church's ignoring of charismatic renewal. It is not the only one, of course, but it is a significant one. Let me explain why. I call this the 'Father Christmas Syndrome'.

When I was young, I was taught that there was a person called 'Father Christmas' who wore a red coat, drove a reindeer-powered sleigh through the sky, and came down the chimney each year to deliver presents from his sack. This seemed to me as a child a pretty self-evident explanation of how the presents got there, and the fact that I never saw him (although I did see men dressed up as him in the shops in the run-up to Christmas) wasn't a problem: built into the story was the fact that he only showed up once we were fast asleep.

But I can remember quite clearly the time when I began to question all this, and the logical gymnastics performed by my parents to deal with my questions. When we blocked up our fireplace and put in a gas fire I was most concerned that no more presents would get through, but I was assured that these days Santa didn't come down chimneys any more, what with all this central heating which everyone was installing. So how did he get in? Through the back door.

This satisfied me for a couple of years, but I can remember asking my mum, 'How can he get in the back door? You always lock it up.' My mum explained that for just that one night in the year everyone leaves their back door unlocked so that he can get in that way.

But by now the rot of questioning, cynicism and unbelief had set well in. What about burglars? Forgive my naïvety but if I were a burglar, and I knew that there was one night each year when everyone left their back doors open, a night indeed when there were piles of loot lying around begging to be burgled, I'd have a field day. No, I needn't worry about that, said Mum. All the burglars in the world had an agreement among themselves that they would refrain from their nefarious activities just for that one night.

But this time I remained unconvinced. When I overheard an episode of *Mrs Dale's Diary* which blew the gaff entirely, I cried at the death of the myth, but I think I had secretly known for some while what a fishy story it all was.

For decades in our church Sunday Schools we have been telling our children stories about a man who wore, in this case, a white coat, and made ill people better, fed huge crowds from a single packed lunch, told adverse weather conditions to stop it, and rose again from death to live for ever. But inevitably there comes an age when questioning sets in. At first it is innocent: as they grow up, children just need to know how things work. But whether the answers are satisfactory or not, the questioning goes deeper and gets more relentless, and above all the desire to experience some of the stuff they've been told about becomes overwhelming. It is at this point, sadly, that the church so often has nothing to give them. Those in the church from a previous generation have either never been through such a questioning phase or have come out the other side and become used to living with the gap between scripture stories and real life. Some of the more thoughtful may even have constructed a clever theology to explain this gap. But for the kids it is just a gap. The Bible is just stories, Jesus is a mythical figure, and it was nice when we were children but now we've got to grow up and get on with real life. So thank you and goodbye, church.

Letting the children in

I remember once hearing a speaker who had a particular ministry among youth who had become involved in occultism and had scared themselves to the extent that they wanted to get free. He noted the disproportionate number of his clients who were ex-evangelical Christians, and he explained his theory as to why this was. Church, he said, had given them a taste for the supernatural and for spiritual power, but then quite simply couldn't deliver the goods. They were told, by implication, that it was all just stories, but they had been hungry enough to begin a search for the super-natural realm elsewhere, and of course there was no shortage of those who could deliver the Enemy's brand of supernaturalism. They were to discover that there was a sting in the tail, but at least it did work. There was experiential reality here which they had quite simply never found in the Christian Church.

A church which takes seriously the supernatural work of the Holy Spirit is, it seems to me, in a position to do something about this tragic state of affairs. If children are allowed right from the start to experience God as well as to hear stories about him, and if the questioning phase can be dealt with honestly by adults who have a working knowledge of the things of the Spirit, this drop-off ought to be almost eliminated. I'm not aware of any formal research on this, but my impression from looking around the church is that charismatic congregations tend to hang on to their teenagers, and that the teenagers they hang on to are far more on fire for God, far more committed to serving him, and much more full of intercessory and evangelistic zeal than others. Many of the mushrooming youth congregations come from a charismatic base, and the health and growth of the most charismatic is impressive indeed.

It was certainly our experience in the parish of which I was vicar that the introduction of charismatic children's ministry halted this drop-off almost entirely. I inherited a church where confirmation was seen as the passing-out ceremony from Sunday School, where the ruling principle was that if you wanted to keep young people you had to cut down on the 'religious' bits, replace them with a profusion of pizzas and ten-pin bowling trips, and then give them a job on the servers' rota. Inevitably almost all of them turned up to church once in six weeks when it was their turn, and were never seen in between. The exceptions tended to be those whose parents were committed members of the church, but even this did not hold true universally.

When Chris, my wife, took over leadership of the children and youth work, she did so with a clear charismatic agenda,[1] and she began steadily to raise the stakes. She began with a confirmation class, where she taught the candidates to pray, listen to God and minister to each other. Within a few weeks all but a couple had left, out of the sheer embarrassment of it all. But Chris is not one to give up easily (she has stayed married to me for twenty-three years!) so she pushed through the pain barrier and kept going.

At the same time she began working with the younger children, for whom the spiritual agenda was nowhere near as difficult. She taught them to pray out loud before they reached the age of five, and many were speaking in tongues and receiving prophetic words and pictures before they started school. As they grew up into the youth group a cultural revolution had taken place, and fully charismatic spirituality was *de rigueur*. By the time we moved on, after nearly eight years in the parish, we left a thriving youth group, from which half a dozen youngsters had gone on to some kind of Christian service or leadership around the country and the world, with a next generation of kids who had moved up through COGS (our name for Sunday School) ready to continue the tradition. Our teenagers were some of the most passionate Christians we have ever seen, heavily involved in the church's life at all levels, and I believe that the kingdom shock-waves from that small group, which started with two almost-committed members, will literally be felt around the world.

Typical of this passion was the time when a group of the youngsters felt that God had spoken to them and told them to use the six weeks of Lent to go prayer-walking around the parish early in the morning. By Easter there was a gang of over twenty of them up every Wednesday at 5.30 a.m., terrorizing early-morning dog-walkers and calling down God's blessings on the parish. Lent came and went, but the prayer continued, until one morning, while walking through the park, they met a man they had never seen before, sitting on a park bench. 'You're Christians, aren't you?' he asked the surprised group. 'You come here once a week to pray, don't you?' he continued. They told him that they were, and that they did. 'Then how come,' he continued, 'you love Jesus enough to get up and pray one morning a week, but I love my dog enough to get up every morning and take him for a walk?' The group mumbled something or other and beat a hasty retreat, but decided from that day on to prayer-walk every day. They never saw the man or his dog again, and are pretty convinced that they encountered an angel on that park bench. Even when we left to move to another city, the prayer went with us. As I write there are representatives from eight city secondary schools meeting first thing in the morning to pray, and there are fervent attempts to get more schools on board.

The teenagers in our new church have just completed a week of 24-7 prayer,[2] a project to keep a constant barrage of prayer for our country going on non-stop, with different churches committing themselves to a week or more at a time, and providing 24-hour prayer for that week. Run almost entirely by young people, this country-wide prayer meeting has been running for a couple of years now, and literally thousands of teenagers have taken part in it. I'm just not sure that without the Holy Spirit's empowering in their lives they could have been bothered. They are certainly bucking the trend of those lentils.

Growing up with God

What caused our youngsters and thousands like them around the country not only to stay in the church but to put most of the adults to shame with their passion and devotion? Chris is convinced that the seeds were sown for that move of God when she began to introduce children as young as 18 months old to the power of the Holy Spirit. Children grew up with a God who actually did things in their lives, a God who worked out in real life the stories they were taught from the Bible, a God whom they felt experientially as well as talked about intellectually. The secondary-school-age drop-off quite literally stopped, and instead we grew a church with many fervent and passionate youngsters serving, worshipping and praying like nobody's business. And the really good news is that of that original confirmation class, several later returned and are still walking with God at the centre of their lives.

People often ask me despairingly how to get youth work going in their church. My answer is always the same: begin in the crèche and wait 15 years. For the sake of those 907,000 lost children, the church needs to get on board with the power of the Spirit as an urgent priority.

Chapter 18

Good News for the Poor?

One of the most common accusations levelled at charismatics is that of 'pietism'. In other words, so the critics say, all they're interested in is having wonderful times of worship, which make them feel good, but they're all so heavenly minded that they're no earthly use. In fact, so the rhetoric goes, in a New Age-obsessed world, where you customize your own religion to give you the maximum buzz and the greatest number of nice feelings, it was inevitable that a Christian equivalent should emerge sooner or later. There's little to choose between the drug-culture and charismatic renewal: all they're about is temporary highs which cumulatively help people to lose contact with the real world. Real Christianity, they continue, connects with the real world, not with some heavenly worship-trip for those in the club. Are there any facts to suggest that charismatics are making a difference in the area of social justice?

Spot the difference

Well, the first thing to say, and although it seems an unimportant niggle I'll say it anyway because behind it lies an important theological point, is that actually there is all the difference in the world between charismatic renewal and the drug-culture. One of the significant things about the Christian faith is that it knows how to do pleasure without a sting in the tail. Many years ago I wrote a book (which sadly never saw the light of day) which contained a chapter on the local church's social programme. I made the point that virtually everything which this world tells us is pleasurable has some kind of negative after-effect: hangovers after parties, credit card bills and possible debt after retail therapy, diets after binges, cancer after smoking, pregnancy, VD or even AIDS after casual sex, and, of course, the distinct possibility of escalating addiction after drug use. The church, I went on to say, is one of the few organizations which knows how to have a good time in a way which completely loses this sting in the tail, and as such we should work hard at an attractive social programme. So even if a good dose of charismatic worship is not all there is to the Christian life, it certainly won't do anyone any harm!

But that said, are there any other criteria by which the health and growth of charismatic churches might be judged, particularly with respect to engagement with the world? Well, I hope that earlier chapters have convinced you of the evangelistic concern and success of charismatics, but what of the more social/justice issues? Are charismatics rolling up their sleeves and getting stuck into the problems of this world? Are they getting their hands dirty among the poor?

Yes, they are, as I shall go on to prove to you, but before I get into my argument proper I do need to make an important preliminary point. In Chapter 16 I talked about ecumenism, and made the point that the kind of ecumenism which is going on among charismatics is of a very different type from that pursued by the official ecumenical committees and organizations, almost to the point of it being unrecognizable as ecumenism to those who have given their lives to the other kind. Charismatics in many places have simply short-circuited the committee-based endeavours of the denominational bureaucrats and have started to work together with other like-minded Christians from other denominations, while retaining their own identities. No attempts are made at the formal reunification of different denominations, which means that no-one has to dot doctrinal 'i's and cross ecclesiological 't's: they just get on, agree enough basics to work together, and agree to differ on the finer points. In the same way, charismatics doing social justice work may look very different indeed from some of their brothers and sisters doing it in other ways – so different, in fact, that they run the risk of being accused of doing nothing at all, because what they do is not being recognized as 'proper' social involvement. Perhaps the most dramatic example of this is the work of Jackie Pullinger-To in the Walled City of Hong Kong, who has seen many hundreds of heroin addicts released from their habits simply by receiving the baptism of the Holy Spirit and the gift of tongues.[1] Understandably, those whose stock-in-trade consists of rehab units, alternative, less addictive drugs and long, slow battles might question the validity of Jackie's work, not least if they don't believe in tongues as a valid manifestation of the Holy Spirit for today. Similarly, the call of John Mulinde to 'fill the nation of Uganda with prayer', particularly over the AIDS crisis, resulted in Uganda being the only African country in which the AIDS rate is falling, and falling at the fastest rate anywhere in the world.[2]

There is charismatic social work going on, but it may differ considerably from non-charismatic equivalents. I think that there are different reasons for this, which we need to understand. The first is to recognize that to charismatics, gifted with a prophetic glimpse of the heart of God, much of the church's social involvement looks as if it simply follows this world's agenda. We have the Campaign for Nuclear Disarmament, so we'd better have *Christian* CND. There's a Green Party for the environment, so we need a Christian Green organization. Surely, say the charismatics, we should be setting some of the agendas, not just following the world's? What about the issues which are not politically sexy, but which in God's sight might just be the most important, like the breakdown of family life, and greed and consumerism, and the mass abandoning by our nation of traditional biblical morality, and even a party-political system built firmly on the ability to slag off your opponents at every opportunity? Aren't some of these issues worthy of our attention?

Starting with the gospel

But it isn't just the content which might be different. What about the motivation? Some Christians have been accused of driving a wedge between evangelism and social concern, and of concentrating on one at the expense of the other. This may be unfair, but there really can be significant differences in the end from which you come at it. Christians of a more liberal persuasion might say that social concern comes before evangelism, that people won't hear your gospel if they're in pain, or hungry, or homeless. We must feed the poor in order to win the right to evangelize them. Others, even more radical, would assert that when we feed the hungry we are doing evangelism: God isn't that interested in whether people make some kind of a faith decision, but he cares deeply about their standards of living. So to do his will, we must work with the poor to alleviate their misery. That is evangelism worth the name.

But charismatics would disagree, seeing these two views as far too earthbound. Our job is not just to make people's ride to hell more comfy, but to ensure that they have decent living conditions now *and* an eternity secure with God. So charismatics tend to begin from the gospel end, seeing social justice as a necessary adjunct of that, rather than beginning with social issues and adding the gospel of personal salvation and reconciliation to God later or not at all. They would claim precedent for this from church history, pointing first and foremost to the Wesleys, who set out to preach the gospel but changed the face of Britain in the process. As a result of the mass conversions to Christ which John's gospel preaching brought forth, trade unions were invented to protect the rights of workers, and football was instituted as a sport as a humane alternative to the then popular bear-baiting (there are those who think we need a new revival nowadays to bring in a humane alternative to football). General Booth is another hero whose gospel preaching led to massive changes in society and ongoing social action projects by the Salvation Army (note the name) today. And, of course, the effects on crime rate, drinking and family life of the Welsh revival are well documented. On the other hand, charismatics might look at some of those working so hard in the worlds of politics, social work and so on, and ask, 'What have you actually achieved of significance on a national level?' Rightly or wrongly, many charismatics believe that to begin with the gospel means that you have people put right with God and changes in the way society behaves, whereas those who major, perhaps exclusively, on justice issues seem to have managed very little in the way of national change. And if you asked them for biblical proof that this approach is the right one, you might well be pointed to Isaiah 61:11, a favourite verse:

> For as the soil makes the young plant come up
> and a garden causes seeds to grow,
> so the Sovereign LORD will make righteousness and praise
> spring up before all nations.

Righteousness will come via the praise of the charismatics, so they believe, and not from the anger or cynicism of the social-gospel people, or even from the guns of the liberation theologians.

Who are the poor?

Content, style, but what of the recipients? Just who are the poor? Again, the charismatics might disagree with others, believing that it is a mark of the consumerism and materialism of our society that we define the poor almost exclusively in financial terms. I can remember clearly when I worked in Sheffield, one Saturday after we'd been out for the day, nipping down to the corner shop for something or other and overhearing a conversation about some tremendous crisis which had just happened. I asked what was going on, and I was told about the Hillsborough disaster, about two miles from where we were, where 96 bodies had been crushed and mangled to death. As a church we had major hands-on involvement in the aftermath of that Saturday, but the most interesting thing was that we as a staff team, in seeking to pray about the whole situation from God's perspective, felt very clearly led to pray for the police who, God told us, were 'the poor' in this situation. A policeman wasn't a good thing to be on the streets of Sheffield for a good while after that, but our ministry, we felt sure, was to the police, who were cast in the role of collective villains of the piece. To think creatively about who exactly constitute the poor, and not just to work from the amount of money people have, is a creative insight which we badly need. This is also helpful to those whom

God has called to work in places other than the inner cities. When I left college, after having the 'urban world' and its needs drummed into us day after day, there was a kind of snobbery going on as to who could find the worst parish to go and work in, with the worst housing, the highest infant mortality rates, and so on. The grottier the area, the better a priest you were to go and live there. (In defiance of this silly game, I went to rural Norfolk, which was every bit as spiritually tough, even if we didn't get burgled once a week.) When I went to be the vicar of a posh suburban parish, where Rollers, Porsches, Mercs and even the odd Ferrari abounded, I deliberately took the line of finding out who were the poor in that parish and not of beating myself up because I had not ended up in inner-city Manchester or somewhere. Among our poor were the lonely divorced, left with the kids behind their conifer hedges and block paving, but desperately hurting inside and unable to admit it to anyone in our proud, self-sufficient little community. It isn't just lack of money which makes you poor.

Words – or actions?

So there are some introductory explanations which may or may not have convinced you, but what of the facts? What is actually going on out there, and are renewed Christians showing any significant involvement which makes all that more than just rhetoric?

Remembering our world-wide perspective, we must first note that pentecostal/charismatic spirituality is a movement among the poor, and as such reflects the ministry of Jesus. Charismatics in much of the world are getting on and doing what much of the middle-class British church is only agonizing about not doing. While we work hard but ineffectually at bringing the gospel to our inner-city Urban Priority Areas and our rural farming communities decimated by government policies, in other parts of the world the common people are hearing Jesus gladly and finding strength and hope to live in crushing poverty but with the light of life shining from their eyes. The middle-class agenda of liberation theology, to free people from their poverty, seems to be welcomed much less than the Pentecostals' efforts to give people resources to cope within their poverty. Sadly we have not yet managed this degree of involvement with the poorest people of Britain, but world-wide charismatics are often at the forefront of social justice issues. In Latin America, for example, there is evidence to suggest that the experience of renewal among the poor has freed many from the de-skilling domination of the Catholic priestly class and empowered them to begin contributing on a spiritual level (through a prayer or prophecy). This in turn has given people confidence to begin to speak out against injustices in society. As the Roman Catholic Church has withdrawn more and more from the justice issues which were traditionally its domain, the work is being done instead by the Pentecostals. Jean-Jacques Suurmond argues this forcefully in his book on charismatic renewal, *Word and Spirit at Play*.[3] The story of his call first and foremost to the poor is told by Carlos Annacondia, an Argentinean businessman-turned-evangelist, and one of the key figures in the Argentine revival.

> My ministry began among the very poor, in very humble neighbourhoods, where I would visit hospitals to pray for the sick. I struggled mightily at the beginning because I was unsure whether the Lord wanted me to give up my business and all my worldly possessions. I seemed to hear the voice of God telling me 'Your heart is still set on your things.'
> So I said 'Lord, use me! Use me!'
> And God answered, 'Go to the slums, and give me your business.'[4]

Annacondia now leads immense evangelistic crusades, in Argentina and around the world, where thousands have responded to his gospel preaching, healing ministry and deliverance. From those beginnings in the slums, the face of a nation has been changed. The poor feature heavily in the growth of pentecostal Christianity in Latin America.

But where Roman Catholics are embracing renewal spirituality there is still significant social involvement. A video called *Viva Christo Rey!* tells the story of a Catholic church on the border of Texas and Mexico which was struck powerfully by its study of Luke 14:13:

> When you give a banquet, invite the poor, the crippled, the lame, the blind, and you will be blessed. Although they cannot repay you, you will be repaid at the resurrection of the righteous.

They decided to obey this command literally, and so took Christmas dinners to the people who lived on the local rubbish tip and spent all day raking through the contents looking for anything they might eat or sell. They grossly underestimated the amount of food they would need, but saw to their amazement that the food was multiplied as they served it. This dramatic example of the miraculous power of God began a ministry to the poor of Juarez which has led hundreds into the kingdom, and seen great strides forward in the alleviation of their poverty.

One major feature of charismatic social concern is the emphasis on 'healing the land', pioneered by people such as Russ Parker and Mike Mitton. The Old Testament emphasizes our need to live in right relationships with God, each other and the land which God has given to us, but the third of these has become neglected in a modernist scientific culture where the created order is simply there for our convenience. It has taken the work of the Holy Spirit through the Green movement to remind us of the fact that, according to the Bible, God's redemptive purposes are not just for people but for all creation. In the past our relationship with the land has been broken as we've decimated the rain forests and many species of animals who live there, eroded a hole in the ozone layer and poisoned great tracts with our chemicals. But more significant still is the discovery that a place which has seen evil and violence can become wounded, but can be healed through the redemptive power of God. Discovering Cain's murder of his brother Abel, the Lord said, 'What have you done? Listen! Your brother's blood cries out to me from the ground. Now you are under a curse and driven from the ground' (Genesis 1:10–11). The promise of 2 Chronicles 7:14, something of a purple passage for charismatics, states significantly that the result of humble prayer and repentance will be both the forgiveness of sins and the healing of the land. Some charismatics have done a significant amount of work on discovering the nature of wounds on the land, and through prayer, vicarious repentance and reconciliation, have seen some degree of healing for the community as a whole.

There is also a significant amount of work being done through the ministry of reconciliation, a ministry which has caught the secular public eye to some degree as moves have been made to apologize on behalf of one nation to the people of another for atrocities carried out in the past. Land has been restored to peoples from whom it had previously been snatched, and better relationships have ensued. Of course, this is not just the work of charismatics: Coventry Cathedral, near where I used to live and work, has specifically felt itself called to a ministry of reconciliation, particularly with some European cities where there was mutual bombing during the Second World War. But in many places charismatics are in the forefront of identificational repentance, apologizing for the sins and cruelty of the past and seeing God's *shalom* in terms of healed relationships. Racism in the Southern states of the USA is still a very live issue, but much work is being done to heal and forgive the wounds of the past.

Meanwhile, back in Britain ...

All this is very grand, but what about yer average British charismatic church? Again, I am convinced that rather than the pietism of which charismatics are so often accused, there is a significant degree of social involvement going on through local churches. When I'm not jaunting around the country I attend a medium-sized Anglican charismatic church in the Midlands. Under the general heading of its 'Mercy Ministries' are to be found such projects as the Prospects Group, providing a safe small-group environment for people with learning difficulties; the Friendship Group, working among the elderly; and Little Nippers, primarily a parent-and-toddler group, but which works with adults running parenting courses and so on. Meanwhile the young people are raising money and awareness of Hope HIV, a charity which had its roots within the Salvation Army and which now provides orphanages for HIV-positive babies and children in South Africa. A team of youngsters is also currently working on a mission in Buenos Aires, Argentina.

One couple feel God's call to minister to the needy in a poorer corner of the parish, with a view to planting a house for homeless people and even a church congregation there. But the greatest single area of growth is in the Storehouse, a ministry which began simply by providing food and clothing for hungry or homeless people but which has now formed itself with a group identity. Christians are involved with the people who come, many of whom have drink- or drug-related problems, in all sorts of ways: providing a free hairdressing service, helping those who are released into the community to set up home with the practicalities of doing so, and of course lots of one-to-one counselling. In March 2000 the group was recognized by the local Social Services department and achieved referral status. In response to sudden and rapid growth (from a steady 15 contacts at the outset to over 80 a year later) the church has decided to pay a part-time member of staff to oversee this area of the church's life. And, of course, all this is on top of the church's normal support for mission partners and parachurch organizations engaged in evangelistic, renewal or social issues at home and abroad.

This is not to boast about my church (anyway it isn't 'mine'; I just go there when I can) but to make the point that we are not at all atypical of local charismatic churches. In his 'state-of-the-art' review of the charismatic movement, Nigel Scotland lists many areas in which charismatic local churches are working among 'the poor'. His list includes schemes for the unemployed at Anfield in Liverpool and in South London with Ichthus; education and play schemes; Christian schools which seek to bring Christian principles to bear on both the curriculum and the total school experience, and which are open to the children of parents who are not Christians or members of the church (examples are to be found in Witney, Basingstoke, Gloucester and Worcester). Scotland notes that many renewed congregations have involvement with other churches or with projects overseas. Bristol Christian Fellowship have links with Zambia and South Africa. New Frontiers International have congregations and work in India; Coventry Christian Fellowship, alongside other Coventry churches, work in Albania. Stroud Christian Fellowship have established a pregnancy crisis centre.

Dr Patrick Dixon from the Pioneer network launched ACET (AIDS, Care, Education and Training) in West London as a Christian response to HIV/AIDS. Two London Vineyard churches have shown a great deal of practical care for the homeless and hungry on the London embankments. The Courage Trust is a London-based organization run by charismatic Christians who help to rehabilitate homosexuals who want to change to a heterosexual lifestyle. An Anglican church in Bath has sent mission teams and aid to South Africa, the Middle East, Croatia and Uganda. Members of St Thomas' in Sheffield have driven trucks full of goodies to Bosnia; St Andrew's Church, Chorleywood, is active in fund-raising and other projects for the homeless in London. Pioneer People in the Wirral are working with a partnership project in Albania. Members of Petersfield Christian Fellowship, who have been actively concerned for children in Colombia and South America, have formed a charity known as In Ministry to Children. Salt and Light Ministries have their own worldwide arm, CRI (Church Relief International), which channels money and personnel into practical relief. River Church, which is part of the Pioneer network, purchased a large house for the homeless in the early 1990s; Pioneer also established Romania Aid, based at Cobham in Surrey. In 1974 Myrtle and Cecil Kerr founded a Christian Renewal Centre at Rostrevor in Northern Ireland where a community of Roman Catholics and Protestants work together for renewal and reconciliation. At the 1999 Stoneleigh Bible Week, £300,000, part of a collection, was set aside for ministry to the poor. Many charismatic Christians are active supporters of CARE and the Evangelical Alliance, both of which are deeply involved in the socio-political arena. Significantly, their directors, Lyndon Bowring and Joel Edwards, are both charismatic Christians. Many charismatic churches have also been active in the Jubilee Campaign to 'Keep Sunday Special' and in Christmas Cracker, which raises money and sends gifts to poor children in developing war-torn countries. Other congregations have given support to Baroness Cox and Christian Solidarity International. Scotland comments:

> These organisations and initiatives are a representative selection of the social activities in which charismatic Christians are actively involved. They are indicative of the growing social concern for the wider world on the part of charismatic churches.[5]

It may have been true in the early days of renewal that Christians seemed more interested in getting blessed than in blessing others, but things have moved onward and outward since those days. As theologian Mark Stibbe notes:

> In the final analysis, any pneumatology or doctrine of the Holy Spirit which is purely concerned with the work of the Spirit in the church, or, worse still, in us as individual Christians, is hopelessly myopic. The Holy Spirit is concerned not only with our own liberation, but also with the liberation of societies, cultures, nature and indeed the whole cosmos.[6]

And of course the gospel to the poor is happening on a scale wider that just that of the local church. As I'm writing this section my two teenage sons are away in Manchester at Soul Survivor which, in 2000, decided to meet not in a field in Somerset but in a park in Manchester. Under the motto 'A message of love and a demonstration of love' the mornings are filled with teaching and worship, and then the participants are dispersing into different parts of the city to take part in street evangelism and community projects, such as creating play-spaces out of derelict land or cleaning up deserted houses in the worst estates in order to make them habitable again.

But this is just the cutting edge: less noticeable to the public view is the Eden Project, where Christian couples and families are moving into some of the worst Manchester estates in order to live and work among the poor of the city. Eden was noticed by Christopher Middleton, a reporter for the *Daily Telegraph*, who asks in the property section, 'Could these people raise your house price?' and tells the story of 60 or so people who have given up highly paid jobs in other parts of the country to move into Salford and Wythenshawe. These settlers believe they have done their bit, alongside urban regeneration projects, to repair the social fabric.

'I really do think we have helped, not least because we've been prepared to stand up and be counted' says Anna [one of those who has
made her home in Wythenshawe] ...

'We've been to court on behalf of people, and we've been to court
against these self-same people. And that makes an impression in an
area where so many kids have simply not been taught the difference
between right and wrong.'

Andy Hawthorne, an Anglican and leader of the World Wide Message Tribe, a Christian dance and rave outfit, notes that

For every place on the scheme we get at least 10 applicants ... who
are prepared to live in a slum for low wages.

Most of us have tried living solely for ourselves and have found it
doesn't work ... that's the thing about living for other people – until
you've tried it you've no idea of just how exciting it is.[7]

Transforming the world

In some places of the world, however, renewal has gone even
further than this. The Holy Spirit comes not just to gift the church
and to help Christians have deeply meaningful times of worship: he
comes to transform whole communities with the power of the
gospel. A video called *Transformations*[8] is currently exciting
the charismatic world. Based on studies by George Otis Jr, it tells
the stories of four communities which have seen the miraculous
renewing power of the Spirit begin to affect much more than just
the church.

Cali in Columbia was one of the illegal drug capitals of Latin
America. Following the murder of a church leader who dared to
speak and pray against the drug barons, explosive church growth
took place in the city. The church had been typically mediocre, with
an average congregational size somewhere around the 65 mark.
Murders ran at an average of 15 per day (in the whole city, that is,
not the church), but after the assassination virtually every church
began to grow. The largest now has 35,000 members, and the sheer
number of Spirit-filled Christians has begun to affect the spiritual

atmosphere of the city. Over one whole weekend, when there was a massed prayer gathering, the secular press reported that there had not been one single murder during the weekend, and many of the drug cartels have been smashed by the power of prayer. Not surprisingly, many of the political leaders of the city have come to respect and even to join the Christians.

Kiambu is a suburb of Nairobi in Kenya, famous for having the highest crime rate in all the nation. Much of the crime was the result of epidemic alcoholism (over 90 per cent of the adult population), and as far as the church was concerned the place was a ministry graveyard. No church had ever been able to grow into treble figures. But then praying Christians had felt God directing their attention towards a witch who had great spiritual and political control over the life of the community. As a result of their intercession she was arrested and thrown out of town. Very quickly church growth began, alcoholism dropped, people learned to stay sober and therefore to hold down jobs. This eliminated much of the crime which happened out of sheer boredom, and it enabled families to hold together and to be provided for properly. The church now numbers 5,000 members, and the whole reputation of the area has been turned around. People are even trying to move into the area because of its new prosperity.

Hemet in California was one of the great cult-centres of North America. It was a centre for the manufacture of illegal drugs, and attracted to it occultists and cult leaders like flies round something nasty on the pavement. Gang warfare and vandalism characterized this wounded community, until the Holy Spirit moved in in power. People were spontaneously encountered by the Spirit of God and brought to conversion, and the church now numbers 14 per cent of the population. Christians make up 30 per cent of the police force, and an even higher proportion of those involved in education. Many of the political leaders are Christians also. Crime is on the run, and the newly renewed church is continuing to grow through its ministry of feeding and clothing the poor of the area, and providing free medical care.

But the most amazing story comes from the town of Almolonga in Guatemala. Ruled in the past by a syncretistic combination of superstitious Catholicism and ancestor-worship, it now boasts 80 per cent of the population as Christians. In a town where poverty, alcoholism and domestic violence provided a vicious cycle of crime and hopelessness, the handful of Christians were despised and persecuted. But following united prayer the church discovered the power of the Holy Spirit to heal the sick and deal with those affected by the demonic world. Many people began to find faith, with a resultant drop in crime and violence rates. Eventually all four jails in the town were closed down, since they were no longer needed. But even more dramatic was the resultant change in the very land itself. What work there had been in the community was based around growing and selling vegetables. About four truck-loads of vegetables were exported each month. But the more the church grew, the faster and larger the crops began to grow. Currently they have four harvests each year, and the four trucks per month has risen to 40 per week. The video shows farmers holding carrots at least 18 inches long, stretching from elbow to finger-tips. A crop of radishes, which has always taken 60 days to grow, now comes to fruition in just 25 days, prompting a group of government scientists to visit the town to try to explain this amazing phenomenon. Needless to say, the locals were less than helpful: all they could put it down to was the power of prayer. God was literally blessing the land.

These four stories are typical of many from other parts of the world, where as a result of united prayer on the part of the church God has poured out his Spirit, not just upon Christians but also on the community as a whole. The result of this in every case has been not just church growth, but a church alive to God through prayer and fasting, and alive to the community through care for the poor and political involvement. And it is fascinating to note that even in the most rapidly growing churches there is no sense of resting on laurels: the more a church grows the more concerned it seems to be for the life of the whole community.

It was my great privilege recently to be invited to a consultation in Cape Town, South Africa, on 'Transformed Communities', where we heard from George Otis and other key players in some of the cities featured in the video, as well as many others from cities at different stages along the transformation process. It was a truly inspiring gathering: Otis has fully documented over 40 such communities, and he is aware of at least as many again which he has not yet been able to research fully. This is not a new phenomenon, but in his opinion the rate at which it is happening is absolutely unprecedented in the history of the church. Watch this space!

We've been asking the question 'Why should I be charismatic?' One answer is that to embrace this spirituality might just be a good context from which to obey the gospel imperatives to bring, and to be, good news to the poor.

Epilogue
....

Responding to the Spirit

Congratulations! You've made it this far through the book, and I hope you've found it interesting, maybe even illuminating. I've tried to the best of my ability to prove to you that the life and power of the Holy Spirit is something which God wants for you, and that to open yourself to him will, in all sorts of ways, do you good. Some of my arguments will, no doubt, have been more convincing than others, and you may still have lots of questions, but I hope that something somewhere within you has said 'Yes!' to this book. So what do you do now?

I try to make it a principle whenever I'm preaching to build in the opportunity for some kind of a response.[1] So it seems appropriate to end this book in the same way, although of course it will be much more difficult through the written word to an anonymous collection of readers, most of whom I will never meet.

There might be all sorts of different scenarios. You may, for example, have been intellectually convinced by my stunning arguments. When I said 'Yes' to the Spirit 25 years ago I was, like C.S. Lewis surrendering to the claims of Christ on his life, a very reluctant and dejected convert. I wasn't at all keen on this charismatic stuff, but I knew in my head that it was right, and that it made the best sense of what the Bible appeared to me to be saying. I submitted as an act of will, even though I was emotionally pretty terrified.

Or, on the other hand, it might be for you the other way round. Frankly, you're not sure. You're very grateful to me for having taken the time to write this book and explain it all to you, but those arguments? Well ... pretty weak in places, to be honest. A bit more thinking to be done before you swallow it all. And yet ... something in you wants to respond. You can't perhaps put your finger on it, but you've got in touch with a bit of a yearning, a touch of wistfulness for more of God. A sneaking feeling, no more than that, that renewal might be something you've been searching for, without having articulated it, for a while. You may know some charismatics, and while you hate a lot of what they do and stand for, you can't deny a certain grudging respect, as if they've got something which you haven't.

Or this might be between you and God. You've perhaps been aware for some time that he's been calling you forward, into some kind of a next step. Reading this book may have been a part of that journey. You don't feel you understand it all, and you're certainly not sure you want it all, but it does seem to make some sense, and it feels as if there might be some continuity with the journey God has been taking you on for a while. At the very least you feel, perhaps a bit nervously, that at the very least you want to walk with God a bit further in this direction.

The next step

So without signing up here and now as a fully fledged charismatic, how do you proceed? The most obvious answer, of course, is that you find your nearest charismatic church and turn up asking for someone to lay hands on you for baptism in the Spirit. Well, that's fine if that's where you're at, but I suspect most of my readers will be a long way from there. Is there a simpler, less demanding and less public way forward? The answer, I suspect, has to do with thirst. The most crucial thing is for you to want more of God, and more of what he has for you.

God had more for a young girl called Mary – quite a lot more, in fact. As a devout Jewish girl she was no doubt seeking to live in obedience to the Law, worshipping at the synagogue, reading the scriptures, and so on. But one day she was visited by an angel. Not just any old angel, but one of the senior management. Once she'd recovered from the shock, she listened to what he had to say, as you would. God wanted to give her more. In fact, he wanted to plant in her womb his very own son, so that he could live as a human being among the people whom God loved so much. This baby was to be both human and divine, and the conception was to be a miraculous combination of her body and the Holy Spirit. What do you say, Mary? Is that OK with you? Mary had to make a response, and however long it took her to make up her mind, however much of the conversation is not recorded for us by Luke, she arrived at the place of surrender. 'I am the Lord's servant,' Mary answered. 'May it be to me as you have said.'

Now I'm not for one moment suggesting that being filled with the Spirit comes anywhere near Mary's task in its significance or in the momentous nature of its implications. This was literally a unique event, whereas I've argued throughout this book that baptism in the Spirit is (or should be) perfectly normal and natural. But the key lies, I think, in Mary's response. God was asking for more of her devotion, and at the same time he was wanting to give her more of himself. It would change everything: there was no way she could simply carry on as before. No doubt she thought about the social stigma of being an unmarried mum, the responsibility of having and caring for a baby – and not just any baby, but the Son of God himself. Maybe she fantasized about how she'd tell people, and the knowing winks behind her back which said the Aramaic equivalent of 'Pull the other one!' This wasn't a decision you reached easily or quickly. And yet, all things considered, she said yes to God. 'May it be to me as you have said.'

Becoming charismatic, or even moving towards becoming charismatic, might seem to you a huge step to take. Believe me, I know. I've been there. But without a decision to submit to God and open up to him, whatever the cost, you'll simply stay where you are.

Thirsting for God

So what is it that might make you want to take that outrageous step? Simply, as I've already said, a thirst for more. You've probably experienced times when you've felt so close to God that you could almost reach out and touch him: at such moments, possibly in the context of worship, you've felt that there's nothing you'd like better than to stay with him for ever. And then you've probably come to, and the feeling has faded, and life has gone on as before, the incident quickly forgotten. The secret of openness to the Spirit is to seek and cultivate such times when things get for a few moments into a right perspective and you really do want God with all your heart, mind, soul and strength.

Many of the psalmists knew what that felt like: outpourings such as

O God, you are my God,
earnestly I seek you;
my soul thirsts for you,
my body longs for you.

(Psalm 63:1)

and

One thing I ask of the LORD,
this is what I seek:
that I may dwell in the house of the LORD
all the days of my life,
to gaze upon the beauty of the LORD
and to seek him in his temple.

(Psalm 27:4)

are not uncommon. It is this thirst, this sense of the emptiness of life without God, which is an essential prerequisite for receiving more from him, and being willing to surrender more to him. Some of the people who have read this book – not everyone, by any means, but some – will have been feeling such a thirst for more of the Holy Spirit, and if that's you I want to encourage you to pursue it. Pray for God to pour out his Spirit on you: spend time before him in prayer and worship, and, yes, even ask others to pray for you if you feel brave enough. There are no magic formulae, just a determination to wrestle with God and not to let go until he blesses you.

My hope and prayer is that for some who have read this book it will have been a gateway into a new dimension of life as a follower of Jesus. For others it might have answered some questions, or made things a little clearer, and that's great, but my real desire is to see Christians grabbing hold of everything God has for them through the Holy Spirit, being filled with his power, eagerly desiring his gifts and growing in his fruit. So go for it!

Notes

....

Introduction: Why Should I Read This Book?

1 Mitton, M. (ed.) *The Way of Renewal* (London: Church House Publishing, 1998).

2 See Matthew 12:22–32.

1 Confessions of a Reluctant Charismatic

1 Otto, R., *The Idea of the Holy* (Oxford: OUP, 1923).

2 Take Your Pick!

1 Personally I hope very much that they were right with regard to AIDS: I'm not against science, and I'm not ungrateful for the tremendous discoveries we've made. I'm just illustrating the blind faith which we put in science as the curer of all our ills.

3 What Is This Thing Called 'Charismatic'?

1 Wimber, J., with Springer, K., *Power Evangelism* (London: Hodder and Stoughton, 1985) pp. 151ff. This section is a short summary of the research written up in Wimber's *Signs and Wonders and Church Growth* conference manual.

2 This estimate comes from S.M. Burgess, G.B. McGee and P.H. Alexander (eds) *Dictionary of Pentecostal and Charismatic Movements* (Grand Rapids: Zondervan, 1988) p. 813. See p. 160 for the actual figures.

4 Charismatic Spirituality

1 McDonnell, K., *Presence, Power and Praise: Documents of the Charismatic Renewal* (Collegeville, Minnesota: Liturgical Press, 1980).

2   Colin Buchanan, *Encountering Charismatic Worship* (Nottingham: Grove, 1977) pp. 10, 13.
3   John Goldingay, 'Charismatic Spirituality – some theological reflections' in *Theology* 99 (1996) pp. 178–87.
4   John Leach, *Living Liturgy* (Eastbourne: Kingsway, 1997) pp. 15f.
5   Colin Urquhart, *When the Spirit Comes* (London: Hodder and Stoughton, 1974) p. 12.
6   See my *Hymns and Spiritual Songs* (Cambridge: Grove, 1999) for a fuller discussion of the differences between hymns and worship songs.
7   Robert Warren, *Being Human, Being Church* (London: Marshalls, 1995) p. 119.

5 In at the Deep End

1   Pawson, D., *The Normal Christian Birth* (London: Hodder and Stoughton, 1997). See also James Dunn's earlier *Baptism in the Holy Spirit* (London: SCM, 1970).
2   Turner, M., *The Holy Spirit and Spiritual Gifts Then and Now* (Carlisle: Paternoster, 1996) p. 135, quoting G. Fee, *God's Empowering Presence* (Peabody, Mass.: Hendrickson, 1994) p. 898.
3   *Ibid.* pp. 100ff.
4   *Ibid.* p. 168.

6 Blessed Assurance

1   I subsequently discovered that the song is by Paul Crouch and David Mudie, copyright 1989 Daybreak Music, and you can find it in the ICC *Spring Harvest Kids' Praise Songbook 1988/9*.
2   David Pawson, *The Normal Christian Birth* (London: Hodder and Stoughton, 1989, 1977) p. 71.

8 Biblical Theology

1   Schweitzer, A., *The Quest of the Historical Jesus* (London: A. & C. Black, 1910).
2   Notably in his *Parables of the Kingdom* (London: Collins/Fontana, 1961).
3   Cullmann, O., *Christ and Time* (London: SCM, 1960).
4   See J. Wimber, *Power Healing* (London: Hodder and Stoughton, 1986) pp. 62ff. for the exciting account of John's breakthrough.

9 Open to Interpretation

1   A. C. Thisleton, 'The New Hermeneutik' in *New Testament Interpretation* (Exeter: Paternoster, 1979) pp. 308ff, ed. I. H. Marshall.

10 A Very Horrid Thing?

1 Quoted in R.A. Knox, *Enthusiasm* (Oxford: OUP, 1950) p. 450.

2 B.B. Warfield, *Counterfeit Miracles* (New York: Charles Scribner's Sons, 1918).

3 If you are interested in this debate, and feel like tackling some rather scholarly works, try Jon Ruthven *On the Cessation of the Charismata* (Sheffield: Sheffield Academic Press, 1993) or Wayne Grudem (ed.) *Are Miraculous Gifts for Today?* (Leicester: IVP, 1996).

11 Is 'This' 'That'?

1 If you're interested in this area, Max Turner gives it quite a bit of attention in his *The Holy Spirit and Spiritual Gifts Then and Now* (Carlisle: Paternoster, 1996) pp. 303ff.

2 *Ibid.* p. 314.

12 Word and Spirit

1 Deere, J., *Surprised by the Voice of God* (Eastbourne: Kingsway, 1996) pp. 251f.

2 *Ibid.* p. 255.

3 *Ibid.* p. 256.

14 Promises, Promises

1 Wimber, J., *Power Healing* (London: Hodder and Stoughton, 1986).

2 Lewis, D., *Healing: Fiction, Fantasy or Fact?* (London: Hodder and Stoughton, 1989) p. 44.

3 *Ibid.* p. 44.

4 *Ibid.* p. 12. See R. Gardner, *Healing Miracles: A Doctor Investigates* (London: DLT, 1986).

5 Lewis, *op. cit.* p. 21.

6 Lay, G., *Seeking Signs and Missing Wonders* (Crowborough: Monarch, 1998) p. 77.

7 *Ibid.* p. 27.

8 *Ibid.* p. 28.

9 *Ibid.* p. 82.

15 The Death of a Movement?

1 For a sympathetic account of the birth of NOS see R. Warren, *In the Crucible* (Crowborough: Highland, 1989) pp. 215ff. For a detailed and less sympathetic account of its tragic demise, see R. Howard, *The Rise and Fall of the Nine O'Clock Service* (London: Mowbray, 1996).

2 See G. Lay, *Seeking Signs and Missing Wonders* (Crowborough: Monarch, 1998) *passim* for a critique of Cerullo, although if his

comments about Cerullo, whom I do not know personally, are as inaccurate as those about John Wimber, whom I did, they may need taking with a pinch of salt.

3   Hill, C. (ed.) *Blessing the Church?* (Guildford: Eagle, 1995).

4   Glover, P. (ed.) *The Signs and Wonder Movement – EXPOSED* (Bromley: Day One, 1997).

5   Prasch, J.J., *The Final Words of Jesus and Satan's Lies Today* (Cambridge: St Matthew's Publishing, 1999).

6   Philip Foster in Prasch, *op. cit.* p. 5.

7   In Glover, *op. cit.* p. 85.

8   Mark Havill in Glover, *op. cit.* pp. 31f.

9   *Ibid.* pp. 32f.

10 Prasch, *op. cit.* p. 124.

11 Hill, *op. cit.* pp. 186f.

12 Prasch, *op. cit.* pp. 146f.

13 Chris Hand in Glover, *op. cit.* p. 55.

14 Prasch, *op. cit.* p. 94.

15 *Ibid.* p. 237.

16 *Ibid.* p. 228.

17 *Ibid.* p. 152.

18 *Ibid.* pp. 217f.

19 Hill, *op. cit.* p. 105.

20 *Ibid.* pp. 226f.

21 Prasch, *op. cit.* pp. 241f.

22 *Ibid.* p. 227.

23 *Ibid.* p. 111.

24 Porter, S.E. and Richer, P.J. (eds) *The Toronto Blessing – or Is It?* (London: DLT, 1995).

25 Compare P. Dixon, *Signs of Revival* (Eastbourne: Kingsway, 1994) pp. 233ff. with Foster in Glover, *op. cit.* pp. 61ff.

26 From the *Observer*, 4 September 1994, quoted in Dixon, *op. cit.* p. 259.

27 Finney, J., *Fading Splendour?* (London: DLT, 2000) p. ix.

28 *Ibid.* p. 173.

29 *Ibid.* p. 176.

16   If You Can't Beat 'Em ...

1   Bonnington, M., 'Patterns in Charismatic Spirituality' in *Anglicans for Renewal* 83 (2000) p. 32.

2   Source: D.B. Barrett and T.M. Johnson, 'Annual Statistical Table on Global Mission' in *International Bulletin of Missionary Research* 24.1 (January 2000) pp. 24f.

3 Brierley, P., *Future Church* (Crowborough: Monarch, 1998) p. 121.

4 *Ibid.* p. 125.

5 Cox, H., *Fire from Heaven* (London: Cassell, 1996).

6 Cox, H., *The Secular City* (London: SCM, 1965).

7 Cox, H., *Fire from Heaven*, p. xv.

8 *Ibid.* p. xvi.

9 For a more scholarly account of the growth of the New Churches see A. Walker, *Restoring the Kingdom* (London: Hodder and Stoughton, 1985).

10 Brierley, P., *'Christian' England* (London: MARC, 1991) p. 46.

11 Quoted in V. Synan, *The Spirit Said 'Grow'* (Monrovia, Ca.: MARC, 1992) p. ii.

12 Martin, R., *The Catholic Church at the End of the Age* (San Francisco: Ignatius, 1994).

13 Pope John Paul II 'Address to Bishops of Latin America' in *L'Osservatore Romano* (English edn) 21 October 1992, pp. 7f.

14 McDonnell, K. and Montague, G.T., *Fanning the Flame* (Collegeville, Minn.: Liturgical Press, 1991) pp. 20f.

15 Martin, *op. cit.* p. 107.

16 Scotland, N., *Charismatics and the New Millennium* (Guildford: Eagle, 2000) p. 52.

17 Pratchett, T., *Carpe Jugulum* (London: Corgi, 1999) pp. 348ff.

18 Silvoso, E., *That None Should Perish* (Ventura, Ca: Regal, 1994). See also J. Dawson, *Taking our Cities for God* (Milton Keynes: Word, 1989).

19 Riddell, M., *Threshold of the Future* (London: SPCK, 1998) pp. 53f.

17 For the Sake of the Children

1 You can read all about it in J. and C. Leach, *And For Your Children* (Crowborough: Monarch, 1994), now updated and republished as C. Leach, *Children and the Holy Spirit* (Eastbourne: Kingsway, 2001).

2 Information on this project can be found at http://www.24-7prayer.com

18 Good News for the Poor?

1 You can read about Jackie's remarkable work in her *Chasing the Dragon* (London: Hodder and Stoughton, 1980) and *Crack in the Wall* (London: Hodder and Stoughton, 1989).

2 Mulinde, J., *Light or Darkness over Europe* (Seaford: Pillars of Fire, 2000) p. 13.

3 Suurmond, J.-J., *Word and Spirit at Play* (London: SCM, 1994) especially p. 62.

4 Annacondia, C., 'Power Evangelism – Argentine Style' in Wagner, C.P. and Deiros, P. (eds) *The Rising Revival* (Ventura, CA: Renew Books, 1998) p. 61.

5 Scotland, N., *Charismatics and the New Millennium* (Guildford: Eagle, 2000) pp. 317f.

6 Stibbe, M., 'The renewal of harvest – a charismatic theology of creation' in *Anglicans for Renewal* 49 (1992).

7 *Daily Telegraph*, property section, 8 July 2000.

8 *Transformations* is copyright 1999 Sentinel Ministries UK and is available from Sentinel at P.O. Box 11905, London NW10 4ZQ, UK, tel. (+44) 0208 961 6188, gateway@dircon.co.uk. The inevitable *Transformations II* is currently in preparation.

Epilogue: Responding to the Spirit

1 My *Responding to Preaching* (Cambridge: Grove, 1997) deals with this in more detail, in case you're interested.

Index
....